C000319268

the *fastest* man *on* 2 wheels

the fastest man on 2wheels

in pursuit of Chris Boardman

PHIL LIGGETT *and* ANTONY BELL

PHOTOGRAPHY BY PHIL O'CONNOR

BOXTREE

in association with
CYCLING WEEKLY

A Cooling Brown book for Boxtree

First published in Great Britain in 1994 by Boxtree Limited,
Broadwall House, 21 Broadwall, London SE1 9PL

Copyright © 1994 Cooling Brown
Text © 1994 Phil Liggett and Antony Bell

The right of Phil Liggett and Antony Bell to be identified as the Authors of this Work has been
asserted by them in accordance with the Copyright, Design and Patents Act 1988.

1 3 5 7 9 10 8 6 4 2

All rights reserved. Except for use in a review, no part of this book may be reproduced, stored
in a retrieval system or transmitted in any form or by any means, electronic, mechanical, photocopying,
recording or otherwise, without prior permission of Boxtree Ltd.

Edited by James Harrison
Designed by Arthur Brown and Sue Rawkins
Captions by Luke Evans

Colour origination by Daylight Colour Art, Singapore
Printed and bound in Portugal by Printer Portuguesa

A CIP catalogue entry for this book is available from the British Library.

ISBN 1 85283 915 5

Contents

FOREWORD **6**
BY MICK JAGGER

INTRODUCTION **8**

CHAPTER ONE **15**
THE MAN

CHAPTER TWO **27**
THE MACHINE

CHAPTER THREE **39**
THE KEEN EDGE

CHAPTER FOUR **59**
RECORD RETURN

CHAPTER FIVE **71**
POWER OF THE HOUR

CHAPTER SIX **91**
DUEL IN THE RING

CHAPTER SEVEN **99**
TURNING PRO

CHAPTER EIGHT **115**
BEYOND LEVEL FOUR?

REFERENCE SECTION **122**

Foreword

When the Rolling Stones lived in France in the early 1970s, I used to go out on long bikes rides and since those early days, I've used cycling to keep fit, particularly when building up for a long tour. I still have a range of bicycles, including my lightweight road racing machine and some mountain bikes.

It was only by chance that I saw my first competitive cycling event. It happened when I was driving through France. I came across a race and, as the roads were closed, I had to stop. I enjoyed the spectacle and appreciated the effort that the riders put in.

I first saw track cycling in London when the 'Skol 6' six-day event used to be held every September at Wembley. The great Dutchman Peter Post and the "Flemish arrow" Patrick Sercu, added the flair to a great event.

The hour record was not new to me, as quite by chance I was in Mexico in 1984 making a video with the band when Francesco Moser set the record there. I knew what Chris needed to do to be the best.

With information from Alan Dunn I've watched Chris Boardman develop from a noted home champion into an outstanding Olympic gold medallist and in 1993 to the world hour record holder.

When he went for the record in Bordeaux, I was only too happy that we helped him with transport and back-up, and even more pleased when he delivered a result.

Bike racing is the toughest of sports, but cycling is a marvellous pastime – environmentally friendly and a great means of transport. My family all enjoy messing around on bikes and I hope that this account of Chris's amateur career will encourage others to take up the sport, at whatever level.

Chris is now a professional with one of the best teams in the World. I wish him the greatest luck in the seasons ahead.

MICK JAGGER, Los Angeles, USA, 1994

Three years after Mick Jagger witnessed Francesco Moser break the world hour record in Mexico, a British amateur from the Wirral began to realize the potential that would one day lead to an Olympic gold medal and new figures for the prestigious hour record. Chris Boardman is pictured leading the Manchester Wheelers to victory in the 1987 national pursuit championship.

Introduction

THE BRITISH MEDIA ARE AN INSULAR LOT. Give them cricket, rugby, football, horse racing, athletics, boxing and even motor racing, and they can fill any sporting newspaper column or TV slot. But present them with a cycling achievement such as Chris Boardman's gold medal in the 1992 Olympic Games, and they have to find an 'angle': In Boardman's case how to turn his wonderful success into something they could write about and understand. The end result? Boardman's 4,000 metre medal honours was attributed largely to his bicycle and not to his talented legs.

Almost exactly a year later, the Olympic champion was still a Hoylake amateur, but had now gained some credibility with the British media. However, unlike the media in the rest of Europe, none had understood the enormity of the goal achieved by Boardman when he became the first rider to pass the 52 kilometres barrier – smashing the world hour record in the heat of Bordeaux's velodrome in July 1993.

The European press, as crazed about cycling as they are perplexed about cricket, had flocked to witness what they saw as one of the sporting achievements, not of the year, but of the decade. For them it was especially difficult to accept that an amateur rider had broken the professional cycling world's most jealously-guarded record: a record that had been the domain of only the greatest names in cycling sport's hundred-year history.

The French sporting newspaper *L'Equipe* gave four full pages the next morning to Boardman's achievement, while in Britain, television plodded on without a mention, radio transmitted little better and the newspapers by-and-large ignored the new record holder.

At 11:00am on 23 July 1993, Boardman stepped from the track, exactly one hour after the timekeepers had said the words which will stay with him forever: 'Go when you're ready'. He had become the first man to achieve 52.270 kilometres in the hour.

His first words were: 'If I'd real-

Track racing is one of the oldest branches of the sport and the hour record, always set on a banked track, is cycling's most feared and respected event.

Cycling great Eddie Merckx used all the available technology to break the hour record in 1972. His training included riding behind a motorbike at racing speeds on the outdoor high altitude track in New Mexico. Boardman shunned high altitude for his hour record and it is now accepted that a sea level attempt can be just as successful.

ized the importance of this record, I may have thought twice about attempting it.' He was referring to the barrage of knowledgeable questions from an international media who had arrived at the stadium in quizzical mood, hardly prepared to believe that such an achievement at sea level was possible by an 'unknown' rider .

For years, the greatest professional cyclists had talked about attempting to better Italian Francesco Moser's 1984 figures of 51.151 kilometres. But few were prepared to try and fail. However for amateur athletes fear of failure is not so critical: they decide what to do and failure can slip by comparatively unnoticed. This is what happened a week before Boardman made his attempt in France. Graeme Obree, a Scot riding a bicycle completed from parts taken from an old washing machine, attacked and narrowly failed on a new, temporary velodrome in Norway. Only a handful of spectators and

fewer than a dozen media people watched this amateur.

The next day, and because finance for a later attempt would not be available, Obree attacked the record again, so amusing the professional cycling world because they believed no one could seriously recover quickly enough for a second attempt so soon. They were wrong. On 17 July 1993, Chris Boardman learned he was no longer aiming to beat Moser's nine-year-old record, but that of an Ayr amateur who had achieved 51.596 kilometres – adding a further 445 metres to the record.

There was no doubt Boardman would have liked to have been the first to have beaten Moser, one of cycling's most revered figures. Instead he had to be content with beating the less well known Obree. In doing so however, he embarked on a rivalry that you will read about here and which has produced two British world hour record holders – a hundred years after Henri Desgrange, the founder of the Tour de France, established the first record.

The Fastest Man on 2 Wheels is not a full biography of Chris Boardman, but the inspirational tale of an amateur athlete who turned to cycling, having followed in his parents' wheel tracks on Merseyside. Chris's household has always been cycling-crazy and his parents, Keith and Carol, were part of the halcyon days on Merseyside during the 1950s and 1960s when such was the riding strength of the region it seemed everyone was an Olympian or failing that a

Aerodynamics played an important part in Boardman's preperation for the Olympics and world hour record attempt. Wind tunnel testing enabled him and his team to refine existing components but they also confirmed that Chris is one of the most flexible cyclists around today.

Great Britain international. It is not surprising that Keith, and Carol who was also a dedicated club rider, produced an Olympic champion.

When I joined the North Wirral Velo at 18 in 1961 (I joined the club because I liked the name), Keith Boardman was an outstanding time trial rider and those rides slogging many hours over the Llandegla Moors of Wales often reduced me to tears, as I prayed for the moment this tough man would drop into a lower gear and appear, at least, to have the same output as the rest in the struggling pack! But I know there was also a soft side to the tough rider: Keith had to go upstairs as his son prepared to race out the final for Olympic gold as he could not face watching. He knew exactly what his son was going through and the pain of pedalling it with him was too much to bear.

I left the North Wirral Velo to join the Birkenhead North End and eventually the Velo club dissolved. However, thanks to another Boardman it has reformed, modelling the trend of sponsored clubs of the 1990s, taking its membership from far and wide and not mainly from Merseyside.

Like father, like son, perhaps was initially true, but whereas Keith Boardman assumed the perfect familiar life on the banks of the Mersey enjoying local success and stardom around the clubrooms, Chris was slowly drawn into full-time riding as his constant quest to go one step further gradually drew him away from the rest.

Chris was fortunate to meet Eddie Soens, a cycling 'guru' who attracted every top Merseysider to his home, sending them home believing they would become a world champion – that is if you had complied and perhaps dug a little of his garden first! Chris reacted positively to Eddie, and the guru's sudden death, which came soon after a national track championships in 1985, spurred Chris even more. If Eddie had lived to see the Barcelona Olympics in 1992 Merseyside's most respected inspiration would have regarded the gold medal from Chris as a matter-of-fact achievement that was always destined for the young man. Eddie's reaction would have been: 'It's all right tha', now let's think of next season.'

Despite Chris's successes on the British scene, he

lost no friends – not even his rivals – as the quietly spoken Wirralian produced nothing but warmth from relationships born from competition. If he lost he would congratulate his vanquisher, and if he won, he was humble but could still be extrovert enough to tell a good story to the press.

Only since that pivotal Barcelona achievement have I come to really know Chris, 30 years after suffering behind his father's wheels in Wales. By coincidence Chris has also developed a friendship with my Finsbury Park cycling clubmate Alan

Francesco Moser broke the 50km barrier and smashed the hour record in 1984 with his high-tech, low-profile, oversized rear-disc wheeled bike. Boardman believed, wrongly as it turned out, that it would be Moser's record he would be after.

Dunn, which has led to Chris spending much time a mere six miles from my Hertfordshire home.

In December 1993, at the BBC Television Sports Review reception I asked Chris if he would like to go riding with me: 'Well, tomorrow, I would like to go out for three hours and do 75 miles,' he said. I did not continue the conversation, just offering him another glass of water instead!

From a British champion – 30 national titles is a conservative count – to Olympic champion, is a result of 11 years of hard pedalling. When Chris recorded his first time of 29 minutes for a 10-mile time trial near Chester in 1982, there was no indication as to what colour medal, if indeed any, might follow later.

The Fastest Man on 2 Wheels charts Boardman's cycling progress, his influences and mentors, and the high and lows of this remarkable rider. One low occurred just a year before winning the 4,000 metres Olympic title. Boardman finished only fifth – beaten by the Dane Jan-Bo Petersen in the quarter finals of the world championship 4,000 metres pursuit in Stuttgart, Germany. Jan-Bo will remem-

ber that victory as he went on to a bronze medal, and also what happened a year later when he met a much improved Chris Boardman in the quarter finals of the Olympic Games. This time Chris not only caught the perplexed Dane but raced on to a world record of 4 minutes, 24.496 seconds.

Days after winning the Olympic title, Leicester's Saffron Lane velodrome was packed to capacity in the hope that Boardman could add to his new Olympic 4,000 metres title with the world 5,000 metres record.

Under grey, windy skies, and with coach Peter Keen still driving towards Leicester, Boardman decided to attempt the record before the rains ended the meeting. He rode for the crowd who had waited patiently and the result was an astonishing eight seconds' beating of the record (set at altitude by the American Kent Bostick in 1991). His

Breaking the 52kph barrier took dedication, talent and sheer guts from Boardman who won the respect of the whole cycling world after his successful attempt in Bordeaux in July 1993.

5 minutes, 46.025 seconds was a phenomenal achievement on such an inauspicious day.

Later in the changing rooms, 24 year-old Chris stated he had no plans to turn professional – his public was 'out there' and he would race for them – despite his knowledge that as Olympic champion and a world record holder, he was in a position to start negotiating a six-figure starting contract with a leading European professional team.

But such a move would mean spending long periods of time away without his wife Sally and the family. Moreover, top European teams think long and hard before gambling on employing a British export as so many British riders have proved they cannot turn their backs on home for long.

It was not long, however, before Boardman realized that athletes like Linford Christie had much more public and media appeal in Britain in their higher-profile sports, and that any notable increase in the bank balance as a cyclist could only come from mainland Europe – where the public understood the pain and tears of this most demanding sport.

Towards the end of 1993, Boardman accepted an approach from Roger Legeay, the manager of the French GAN team and employer of the American Greg LeMond, three-time winner of the Tour de France. The next step was decided: Chris Boardman, Olympic champion and world hour record holder would turn professional.

Boardman rode his first professional race in Belgium in September 1993 – and won. The Eddy Merckx GP time trial, named after the most famous cyclist who has ever lived, gave Boardman his first taste of big time racing.

No one can doubt the talent of Chris Boardman, and in 1994 he clashes with his professional peers – cyclists who will respect the man who took 'their' record, but who will be out riding against him to take most, if not all, of the spoils. For the quiet and personable cyclist from the North Wirral Velo, his career is just beginning at a school where he gained the highest possible entry certificates but must prove himself all over again. That is certain to be the subject of another book.

PHIL LIGGETT, Lillehammer, Norway, 1994

CHAPTER ONE

The Man

TEN YEARS BEFORE THE GLORIOUS BARCELONA OLYMPICS, Chris Boardman rode his first cycle race. It was in the summer of 1982 and it was the first ten miles of the 100,000 or so he would find himself covering in training and competition in the build up to his Olympic gold medal and world hour record. This first race, on the outskirts of Chester in the north west of England, was a far cry from the intensity and spectacle of the Barcelona Olympics. It was a 10-mile time trial, organized by the club he was later to join, the Birkenhead Victoria Cycling Club, and nobody but the timekeeper and the families of the other twenty or so competitors were present.

Such weekly 10-mile races gave club members a chance either to gauge their fitness or improve their best times. There is no need to enter the race in advance – you just turn up, pay the entry fee (it was 50p in 1982) and race over the out-and-back course, which winds its way through the Cheshire countryside towards the village of Farndon.

Afterwards riders and their families have a drink in the Rake and Pikel, the pub strategically placed on the finish line, where they swap excuses or congratulations before heading off for fish and chips, and home. It is a pleasant evening out for the family while dad or mum, sister or brother, races. This weekly ritual had been part of Chris's life for as long as he could remember.

Chris's parents, Keith and Carol Boardman, are both long time cyclists; their cycling is not just a pastime,

ABOVE: *Bikes have always been a part of the cycling-crazy Boardman household – Chris, at four years, with older sister Lisa.*

OPPOSITE: *Moments after catching Jens Lehmann in the 1992 Olympics 4,000 metre pursuit final, Chris celebrates the first British gold in Olympic cycling for 72 years.*

but an integral part of their lives. They met through cycling, when Keith and two friends joined the North Wirral Velo, a club based across the River Mersey from his home in Liverpool. Keith's romance with club member Carol Linfield wasn't quite like *A Boy, A Girl and A Bike*, the 1940s film which depicted couples cycling along, gazing lovingly at one another. Carol explains: 'The women were just tolerated, really. The club was so male–dominated that I used to go out alone.'

Keith and Carol were married in 1963, and set up home in Hoylake, Carol's home town. Although she raced later, Carol was more of a touring cyclist. It was Keith who raced, competing in time trials, which he fitted around his job as a telephone engineer. Keith's talents were best expressed alone against the clock, over 25 or 50 miles. In the time trial riders start at one minute intervals and are expected to cover the distance alone and unaided. He had tried road racing, where all competitors start together and the first across the line is the winner, but preferred the solo effort, which in France is known as 'the race of truth'.

Shortly after they were married, Keith was shortlisted for the Tokyo Olympics to be held the following year. The selectors thought his talents could be used in the team time trial, where four riders relay each other over a distance of 62 miles. He didn't make the final selection because he felt that his new life as a married man was more important than his sport. 'It was no sacrifice, and it's not an excuse. I had a lovely wife, a nice house and a good job. I was enjoying all that and didn't want to lose any of it.'

Keith's racing and training programme was supervised by Eddie Soens, a man whose occasionally brutal honesty had not endeared him to everybody cycling on Merseyside. Keith and Carol admired and respected Eddie and

their relationship continued through Keith's career. Twenty years later Keith would take his son to meet Soens, and another successful relationship would begin.

Although Keith did not want the pressures of Olympic selection and competition, he wanted to carry on as he had done, racing in time trials around the north of England. Carol continued to go along to support him and in April 1967 Lisa, their first child, was born. Racing continued while Keith and Carol adapted to family life and after the arrival of Christopher Miles Boardman on 26 August 1968 there were three supporters wherever Keith raced.

The family's leisure time revolved around the time trial scene. Races were generally held on Sunday mornings, which meant getting up at unheard-of hours for a six o'clock start, depending on where the race was held. Afterwards the family would go off for the afternoon. 'We always tried to do something with the children after the races – a picnic or swimming or a walk,' explains Keith. A regular stop on the way home was the Eureka Café. A meeting place for Merseyside cyclists since the 1930s, the Eureka is in an ideal location on a crossroads at the beginning of the Wirral peninsular; cyclists from Wirral and Liverpool pass by on their way to North Wales and Cheshire.

Chris remembers those days – the early starts, the bit where his dad disappeared for a couple of hours, and the afternoon activities. His memories are a bit vague when it comes to watching his dad racing. It didn't really mean much to him, but he did know the difference between a 25- and a 50-mile race. 'If it was a 50, it meant I had an extra hour to play before Dad finished the race.' When he was about nine Chris became more aware that not only was

The Eureka Café was, and still is, a mecca for Merseyside cyclists and a gateway to long training rides in North Wales and Cheshire.

Keith riding these races, but he was winning them. He suddenly became interested. 'I used to like standing by the result board, listening to people talking about Keith Boardman and how well he had done.'

Chris was born in Hoylake and, apart from a two year sojourn in nearby Birkenhead, has lived there ever since. A small town on the north west tip of the Wirral peninsula, Hoylake is different from densely-populated north Wirral. Open countryside behind the town and a promenade and beach looking out across the Irish Sea give Hoylake a feeling of space which is enhanced by the views of Hilbre Island and the hills of North Wales. A strategic port 300 years ago, Hoylake's decline has been gradual, from sea port to fishing village to dormitory town.

Chris Boardman grew up here, riding his BMX bike with his friends and spending his school summer holidays at the open-air swimming pool on the promenade, where he would spend the whole day racing the other children up and down the pool. 'I'm sure this helped with my early physical development' he says.

Swimming could have become his sport if cycling had not caught his imagination. Dave Voller, a racing cyclist, has known Chris since they were at infant school together. 'Everything Chris did was planned and calculated,' he says. 'He wanted things to be just right. When we used to go swimming he would race you all the time – he was so competitive.'

Despite the heavy cycling influence in these formative years Chris Boardman had no inclination to take up the sport. His competitiveness was directed into other areas – cross-country running in particular. It was only at the age of thirteen that he began to show an interest in cycle racing. 'I wasn't interested in anything where I couldn't see a

Chris's father, Keith, was a top amateur time triallist in his day and continues to compete as a veteran. He is pictured in the 1964 national 25-mile championship.

natural progression to go on to be a winner – and that's how I saw cycling at first.' In 1982 he started thinking of cycling in different terms. 'I pestered Dad into letting me race in one of the weekly time trials. He wasn't happy about it at first, but eventually agreed to let me ride.'

Keith responds: 'I wanted him to enjoy cycling first, for its own sake. I was worried that if the racing was too hard it would be all that he knew, and he'd pack it in.'

Keith and Carol have never pressured Lisa or Chris into cycling, despite their own love of the sport. Carol explains: 'Over the years we'd seen a lot of parents pushing their children too hard when they were too young.'

They eventually gave in to Chris's persistence, and he rode his first race at the age of 13, in June 1982. His time for the distance of ten miles was 29 minutes, 43 seconds – a respectable first performance. He had done no training – it was all down to natural ability and competitiveness. Chris could now see the natural progression he demanded from a sport and began to follow a training programme drawn up by Keith. He joined his parents' next cycling club, the Birkenhead Victoria, and began going out on their weekend rides. By October, the end of his first season, his time for ten miles had improved to 25 minutes, 25 seconds.

There were other, more prominent, clubs than the Birkenhead Victoria, but Chris was intimidated by the stories he had heard about the severity of their training rides. Most Wirral clubs use North Wales for their weekend rides, and places like World's End and Cerrig-y-Druidion sounded daunting to a thirteen year-old, although Chris was not put off for long. 'I realized that a lot of the lads exaggerated how hard the training rides were, and when I went out with them I found it wasn't that bad.' In 1983 Chris moved to the recently re-formed North Wirral Velo, his parents' former club until its demise in the 1960s, and continued to ride time trials, his times improving constantly. By the end of the 1983 season his time for ten miles was 21 minutes, 4 seconds.

Even at this early stage it was clear that Chris had potential. Many insisted that he would have to abandon time trial racing and make the crossover into road and track racing. It is generally accepted in British cycling that a rider with ambition to be a top professional has no future in time trial. This has much to do with the style of racing in continental Europe – where British riders traditionally have gone to develop their careers (and bank balances). There is no time trial scene in countries

such as France, Belgium, Italy and Spain – the only occasion they feature is in multi-stage road races. But in Britain it has become almost a sport in its own right, developing there as a result of mass-start races being banned because of safety aspects by the police as long ago as the turn of this century. It was only in 1948 that mass-start racing resumed in Britain. But the time trial remains popular in Britain because riders of all ages and abilities can compete against each other over the same course. It is a good, wholesome aspect of cycle racing which has thousands of participants each week. Keith was aware of the need for Chris to diversify, but he felt that time trials were an ideal foundation for the future if they were mixed with track and road racing.

In 1984 Chris had his first foray into track racing, at Kirkby stadium on the outskirts of Liverpool. The rider who raced to victory at Barcelona on a bicycle at the cutting edge of technology began his track career on an ancient bike frame which had been rescued from a skip. One evening Keith had taken some household rubbish to the local tip, where he noticed an abandoned bike frame. It looked about the right size for Chris, so it was taken home, and with a new pair of front forks fitted and a kingfisher blue respray, it was ready for action. Keith was never one for fancy equipment – whatever he had in working order would do. If people wanted to judge him, he preferred it to be on his results rather than how expensive his equipment was. Once, in the early 1970s, he was on the start line waiting for the countdown in a 25-mile race. A young rider well-known for his expensive tastes in frames and equipment asked Keith when he was going to get his good bike out. Keith calmly replied that he was sitting on his good bike – then proceeded to win the race! The flashy young rider covered the

ABOVE: *Soens, a former Sergeant in the Tank Corps, fought with distinction as a boxer.*

LEFT: *Eddie Soens stands proudly with one of his charges, Norman Sheil, after Sheil had won the 1959 national championship at the Fallowfield track in Manchester.*

distance in a fashionable – but more pedestrian – manner and didn't mention the subject again.

In May 1984, riding 'the frame from the skip', Chris began racing in the weekly track league at Kirkby. A measure of his early promise can be taken from the result of the north west senior pursuit championship, held in August of that year. By now 'that bike' had been replaced by a proper track bike – one which had been used by former professional, Dave Lloyd, and loaned to Chris by his coach since January, Eddie Soens. Now a 15 year-old juvenile category rider Chris fought his way to the final of this senior championship. His opponent was international rider, Alan Gornall. 'I knew I would win as soon as I started', says

Boardman. 'I just felt that I would do it.' He did, and his coach, Soens, was duly impressed by his young charge. Up until the end of 1983, Keith had guided Chris's career, but he knew his limitations. 'I realized I had taught him all I knew and it was time for somebody else to take charge. Eddie Soens could do much more.'

Eddie Soens was a tough, uncompromising man, who demanded 110 percent effort and commitment from those who came to him for advice. Keith impressed this upon his son. 'We spoke about Chris going to Eddie. I told him it was a big commitment and that it couldn't be treated lightly.' Chris had listened and understood. He knew that Eddie had been involved in the coaching of countless British, European, Commonwealth and World champions, and he also knew about Eddie's hard reputation.

His uncompromising stance often brought him into dispute with the official line of the British Cycling Federation (BCF), some of whose policies and personalities Eddie felt were not in the sport's best interests. His son Bill, himself a former racing cyclist, explains: 'My father would not suffer fools gladly. Everybody knew this, but they also knew that he could recognize physical and mental ability in young athletes, even if they had not yet proved themselves.' Eddie was one of four brothers who were all involved in cycling. As a younger man he had raced in time trials, but gave it up to concentrate on his wife's racing. He devised training plans for Mima, who had many time trial successes, and he later began to look after other local riders.

He had a natural authority, which had been enhanced by his military career. During World War II, when Eddie served in Burma, he was a Regimental Sergeant Major in the King's Own Liverpool Regiment, under whose colours he fought in the boxing ring. His tenacity and pugnacious nature made him a formidable opponent, and he used this experience when he later worked with boxers at Kirkby stadium.

Although Eddie commanded respect from the many riders in his charge, there were occasionally those who couldn't live up to the discipline and high standards he set, and they parted company. He could also be disparaging about others who gave advice, particularly if he felt they were not capable. 'He couldn't coach a bloody frog to jump' was one of the salvos Eddie used to direct at the hapless trainers. Always forthright, Eddie was fond of reminding people: 'It's not a matter of opinion when you are right,' which may give the impression that he had a closed mind or narrow vision but this was not the case. He always wanted to listen and learn to improve his knowledge of cycling coaching. When he worked as a french polisher at Liverpool's Walton Hospital, Eddie would badger doctors for advice on how to deal with a particular injury or illness.

Bill Soens remembers his father Eddie taking him and other young riders to the hospital. 'He had organized blood tests for us with a doctor who was interested in athletics. It was a way of monitoring our fitness level which hadn't been done before in cycling.'

In January 1984, when Keith Boardman took his son to Soens' home in St Helens for their first meeting, Eddie had already seen Chris racing the previous year, so he had some idea of what he was capable of. This first meeting proved what he had thought. As Bill Soens remembers: 'He could recognize certain aspects in a rider, and he saw in Chris the qualities essential to becoming a top-level athlete.' Soens knew that the inner hardness he had detected in Boardman would set him apart from the rest. 'There is not the slightest doubt about it – he knew there was something there; the potential to be a great champion,' says Bill Soens of his father's early days with Chris.

The pugnacious Soens was often at odds with other cycling coaches as well as the UK cycling establishment. No one denied, however, that he had a rare eye for talent – including spotting Chris Boardman's potential.

On one of these first visits to the Soens' house, Chris remembers the discussions about Francesco Moser's world hour record attempt. 'I can remember talking about the attempt, but it was so far removed from me and what I was doing that I didn't really think about it, ' says Chris today. If in 1984 someone had suggested that not one, but two, Britons would go for and beat Moser's record, they would have been laughed out of the room.

From their first meeting the legend, charisma and confidence of Eddie Soens impressed Chris, as did the man's absolute certainty that what he said was right. 'I was very much a follower in those days. I would do what he said, blindly.'

The first of Chris's 30 national championship victories came in 1984, when he won the under-16 10-mile time trial title, with a time of 22 minutes, 16 seconds. There was also a major disappoint-ment that year. Because his times for 10- and 25-mile competitions were so promising, Chris had entered the national junior 25-mile championship, even though he was still classed as a juvenile (a rider under the age of 16). The championship was held on a local course just outside Chester. He finished fifth, behind his local rival, Guy Silvester. The week before the championship Chris had set a new junior record for 25 miles of 52 minutes, 9 seconds. As a juvenile rider, this was a tremendous achievement – but it had an adverse effect. The pressure was on him to win the national race, and he tried to prove he was up to it by riding two races midweek. This youthful exuberance left him drained for the weekend. 'It was my first real disappointment. I really wanted to win it, and I let the pressure get to me.'

Amongst the crowd at the finish of the race was Sally Anne Edwards, a 15 year-old schoolgirl whose father, Barry, and brother, Andrew, were also racing cyclists. She remembers seeing Chris

Dashed hopes – Chris's fifth place in the 1984 national junior 25-mile championship was his first major disappointment. Already his interest in aerodynamics and components was evident and the machine he used had concealed cables, no front derailleur and shoes attached directly to the pedals. Even socks were dispensed with!

for the first time. 'It was after the junior championship race. He didn't win, but everyone said he should have. He was sitting in the back of a car, looking so dejected that I felt sorry for him.'

Chris didn't see Sally that day, and remained unaware of her until she came with her parents to the North Wirral Velo annual dinner and prize presentation that December. He remembers seeing her there: 'I thought she was looking at me, but I wasn't quite sure. I didn't want to do anything about it – I was a bit shy, I suppose.' He didn't speak to her that night, but his friend David O'Brien knew Sally's brother, and had the family's phone number. He was prepared to give Chris the number, but only in exchange for a pair of new Lycra cycling shorts that Chris had received from his new club, Manchester Wheelers. Chris had joined the Wheelers to be able to compete with some of the best riders in the country who had been assembled at the club by Jack Fletcher under the sponsorship of Trumanns Steel. The deal with O'Brien was done, and Chris phoned Sally. Their first date, on Christmas Eve, was in Liverpool's Chinatown. Any possibility of romance was under-mined by the 15 or more club members who were also present. By the time the 1985 season was a few weeks old, Sally was a regular spectator and

Colin Sturgess, a powerful pursuiter with a blistering finish which caught many opponents unawares, arrived in the UK from South Africa in 1985, and shocked everyone by beating Boardman in the national championship.

supporter wherever Chris raced.

In June 1985 Eddie Soens took Chris to Leicester for an open trial for the junior track team. There were no limits – anybody could go along and attempt to prove their worth to the then national track coach, Geoff Cooke. During the trials Chris rode a pursuit race, covering the 3,000 metres six seconds faster than anybody else. The coaches were impressed. It looked as though Boardman would be a certainty for the gold medal in the junior championship later in the year at Leicester – but this was not to be.

The week before the junior championship race in 1985 a 17 year-old rider returned from South Africa, where his family had been living for several years. His name was Colin Sturgess and his victory over Chris Boardman for the gold medal was the first stage of a successful career which culminated in Colin's victory at the world professional pursuit championship in 1989. Keith believes that this (and other) setbacks helped Chris's long-term career: 'They made him the rider he is today. He can deal with disappointment because he has never had things all his own way.'

Despite the disappointments in 1985, Chris's performance in training and his race results meant that he was chosen for the junior world champion-ship in Stuttgart, where he finished seventh in the pursuit race – but he wasn't pleased. 'In a way I felt ashamed. I knew I hadn't really been training hard enough, and I should have gone faster.'

Chris Boardman has always been willing to talk about his plans and objectives to anybody who asks. But at 16 years of age this openness, combined with a belief in himself and his abilities, was often misconstrued. He was thought to be arrogant by some older riders, who felt threatened by a teenager who would give them a hard time in training, beat them in races – and advise them on

Three seniors follow the wheels of Boardman, a junior, on their way to the team pursuit title in 1985. Sadly this was to be the last time trainer Eddie Soens saw Chris in action.

their preparation. 'I had a big mouth and I hadn't really done anything then. It was bound to wind some people up.' And wind them up it did. One former top rider who had raced at the highest level was incandescent with rage when, after a training session in which he had received a drubbing from the teenager, Boardman began to tell him what he should do to improve. It wasn't that Chris set out to offend people – he was just convinced that he had the right ideas and wanted to share them.

Despite this – or perhaps because of it – people began to take notice of the 16 year-old rider. The Soens's influence was making itself felt. Eddie's guidance and motivational skills, combined with Chris's talent, and the excellent support of his parents, meant that his career was becoming one of steady progression. Chris recalls: 'When Eddie said "You can do it", you really believed it.' Twenty five years earlier, Eddie Soens had told Keith Boardman that he could become a champion; 'That was enough for Dad – the fact that Eddie had said he

could be good – but I wanted to see it through.'

Sadly Eddie Soens didn't get the chance to see Chris take his career much further. In August 1985, at the British track championships at Leicester, Eddie suffered a heart attack and collapsed. He was rushed to Leicester Infirmary, where he died following a second attack.

The cycling world suffered a great loss with Eddie's passing. Chris felt this more keenly than most. Despite his many good results during his time with Eddie, he felt it was not enough. 'I felt as though I had wasted his last year. At times the only training I was doing was riding to Sally's house and back.' This feeling of guilt was to have a profound effect on Chris's racing career. During the championship week at Leicester, in the last few days before Eddie died, Chris had represented

Manchester Wheelers in the team pursuit. Although still a junior, his results were good enough for him to be chosen with three senior riders. During one of the heats he had difficulty holding the pace and he couldn't take his turn at the front as the riders relayed each other around the steeply-banked track. Although they defeated their opponents and won a place in the final, one of the team members was angry with Boardman. 'He told Eddie afterwards that I was useless,' says Chris. 'That really motivated me. I didn't want Eddie to agree, so I got my act together.' The final was different. He matched each of the senior members turn for turn, and Manchester Wheelers went on to win the gold medal – Chris Boardman's first senior championship win.

When he learned of Eddie's death, Chris was glad that he had seen him win the gold. 'If we hadn't won it would have meant that the last time he'd seen me race I had failed.'

Keith Boardman remembers the effect that Eddie's death had on Chris: 'He was devastated, but he handled it very well. It was a major hurdle for him, but he eventually got over it.' Keith goes on to say that it was the way Chris dealt with the loss of Eddie that made him realize his potential. 'The inner drive began to show. It was as if his race performances were a tribute to Eddie.'

Although Chris felt that he hadn't done enough under Eddie Soens, his performances during 1985 were good enough to set him apart from his rivals. He had impressed the selectors of the Great Britain track team enough for them to send him to the senior world championship at Bassano in Italy. He was a few days short of his 17th birthday when he arrived in Italy, where he would compete against the world's best riders. It was here that he saw for the first time

Chris on his way to victory in the Weaver Valley '25' in Cheshire. He enjoyed several successes in short-distance hill climb races during this time.

Mike Burrows' Windcheetah prototype bike. He didn't set the world alight at Bassano, but the championship series gave him his first taste of senior international competition. A measure of his consistency and constant progression is that Chris was to be selected for every world championship between 1985 and 1992, as well as the 1986 and 1990 Commonwealth Games, and in 1988 his first Olympics, at Seoul.

After the world championships Chris returned to Hoylake and continued with his time trial successes, his season ending with several victories in the short-distance hill climb races held in October. The following year, 1986, saw Chris win the national junior 25 title at his third attempt. That year also brought his first success in international competition. At the Commonwealth Games, held in Edinburgh, he was a member of the bronze medal winning pursuit squad. Once again he was selected for the world championships, held at Colorado Springs, USA, one month after the Commonwealth Games. In Colorado he rode in the individual pursuit race, where he qualified 24th fastest, with 4 minutes, 48.409 seconds. He also rode in the team pursuit, where Great Britain finished 14th. All of this was valuable experience for the 17 year-old. Following the world championship his season ended the same way as it had the year before, and he began training for 1987.

Just after Christmas Chris was called in by the BCF to take part in tests carried out by a young sports science graduate whose research into race preparation and training had impressed the Federation sufficiently for them to allow him to run tests on their riders. Peter Keen was 22-years old when he met Chris Boardman in January 1987. Neither knew it at the time, but Keen would take the place of Eddie Soens as the guiding influence on Chris Boardman's career. Over the next five years this influence would make itself felt through the gradual progression of Chris Boardman from a promising time trial and track rider to Olympic champion.

But another factor was also to influence Boardman's drive for gold: while Chris developed his ambition to be a rider with great potential, an inventor named Mike Burrows was realizing his own dream of designing the ultimate racing bike: the bike that would become the LotusSport. Would Chris have won

the gold medal on a conventional track racing bike? Fans, journalists, cycling coaches, even Chris himself are happy to speculate on this. But on one thing they all agree: if Chris had won at Barcelona using an ordinary machine, he would not have received a fraction of the publicity that he did using the LotusSport.

Showing the pain of team pursuiting, Chris drops back after doing his turn at the front during the 1986 world championships in Colorado, USA.

*The wheel re-invented – even in silhouette the
LotusSport bike which carried Chris to victory in
the 1992 Olympics stands out as a beautifully
simple yet revolutionary machine.*

CHAPTER TWO

The Machine

ON THE MORNING of Thursday, 30 July 1992, people at their breakfast tables throughout Britain were exchanging views on one of the best stories to emerge from the Barcelona Olympic Games. Together a man and his bike had transformed the record books and taken an Olympic title as well.

It was not so much that Chris Boardman had ended a 72-year drought of Olympic individual cycling success for Britain, but rather that an obscure young man from Wirral had ridden into the glare of international recognition through perfect harmony with a machine. Indeed, after reading the British newspapers at that time, you would have thought it was the bicycle that had covered the 4,000 metres without its rider! But silver medallist, the German Jens Lehmann, put things into perspective when he said: 'It was the man who did it.' Of course it was, but Chris Boardman was the first to admit that the prototype bike, the like of which had never before been seen, played more than its share in panning gold.

The Lotus name helped to capture the imagination of people around the world when Boardman, riding the carbon fibre monocoque bike, won the Olympic title. At this point Lotus had been involved for nine months in a project started ten years earlier by Mike Burrows, an engineer and racing cyclist often described as an eccentric

The team – (from left to right) aerodynamicist Richard Hill, engineer Rudi Thomann, inventor Mike Burrows and Chris prepare for the first wind tunnel tests in the MIRA facility in early 1992.

and occasionally as an inventor. 'As far as I am concerned, with this design I re-invented the bicycle in 1982', says Burrows as he recounts the tale of the development of the bike, which in pre-Lotus days he called Windcheetah because of its aerodynamic qualities.

Burrows was driven to dream up, design and build a new type of bicycle, and believes that before this re-invention there was little that could be done to improve the modern racing bike. It was, he says, 'almost 100 percent efficient.' Essential areas, such as the gears and chain, had been developed to a high standard. Likewise, the standard and quality of racing tyres left little or no room for improvement. At this point Mike Burrows had no Olympic aspirations – he was concerned only with how to enable a bike to be pedalled faster during the time trial races he competed in each week.

Speed is of the essence in this form of competition. The individual races against the clock, over a set distance from 10 to 100 miles, with endurance races over 12 and 24 hours, where the rider has to cover the greatest distance in that time. Although Burrows was prepared to consider anything which could better his performance, there were limits. 'There wasn't much I was willing to do to improve my body, so it had to be the bike.'

Mike realized that he needed something lighter and more aerodynamic, and in December 1982, after some initial research he registered a design with the Patent Office for a bicycle that was essentially an aerofoil on wheels.

There had been many 'new' bicycle designs over the years, all claiming to be revolutionary. There had even been an all-plastic bike, which in sales terms sank as quickly as it did on its publicity-seeking launch, when it was ridden off a ramp into a dock, apparently to reassure potential purchasers that if they wished to do the same, the bicycle would not suffer the problem of rusting. It sank without trace.

Human powered vehicles and the spirit of invention which inspired many of those involved enabled Burrows, a long time HPV fan, to approach the design of a conventional bicycle from a fresh and exciting perspective.

Most of these 'radical concept' bikes were constructed from the traditional steel tubing which was welded together to form the classic bicycle frame shape. What set Mike Burrows' design apart from the rest was the method and material he used to build the frame.

Instead of tubing welded together in the conventional manner, Windcheetah was to be built using a carbon fibre composite which when completed would form a monocoque, or single cell, construction. A textbook definition of monocoque is 'a completely closed thin wall unitary load-bearing shell structure which cannot be analyzed as individual load-bearing members'... Quite. Mike Burrows preferred to describe it as 'a single structured form or shape'. A moulded one-piece monocoque bicycle is very different from the conventional tubular frame which cyclists have used the world over for transport, leisure and competition, and it was through Mike's involvement in an offshoot from mainstream cycling called Human Powered Vehicle (HPV) racing that he took his inspiration for the design.

HPVs are pedalled using a chain and gears but they bear little, if any, resemblance to a bike. The rider sits in a tilted bucket seat and steers the machine with a joystick, which also holds the gear and brake levers. These recumbents can be covered by a body shell, which gives the appearance of a ground level mini-Zeppelin.

Although very popular, HPV racing does not have the authority of the world cycling body, the *Union Cycliste Internationale* (UCI). The design places the vehicles outside the UCI's definition of a bicycle. However, HPVs served a useful purpose for Mike Burrows. Their aerodynamic qualities and streamlined bodies had resulted in some remarkable times being recorded during competition, and gave him an idea. 'I began to wonder why we didn't do something like this in bike design, so I started to design bikes logically, analyzing factors which stopped them going faster.' Nobody had thought like this before – or if they had they didn't do anything about it. Burrows points out that he didn't invent the monocoque: 'I was simply the first person to bring a number of elements together. Moulded bikes had been made before, but I understood the potential for aerodynamics, and I understood what carbon fibre could do.'

Carbon fibre would allow him to build the bike directly to whatever shape was required in the quest for maximum aerodynamic effectiveness, and Burrows decided to use his latest steel tube frame design as a model for the monocoque.

In his search for pure speed in time trialling, Burrows had designed – before his monocoque idea – several steel tube framed bikes which incorporated the latest ideas of wind resistance reduction. The 'low profile' bike, so named because the top tube or crossbar sloped downwards from the seat to the handlebars, was intended to reduce the frontal area of the rider, putting them into a more aerodynamic position. There is some disagreement over where this idea originated; some point to the former East Germany – always at the forefront of cycling technology – while several British frame builders claim the idea as their own. Wherever the design came from, a low profile bike was *de rigeur* for every self-respecting time triallist during the early 1980s. Prior to this development, time trial bikes were essentially road racing machines stripped down to the minimum.

Weight saving was thought to be the answer before the importance of aerodynamics was realized. Some took this to extremes and began to drill and cut out what they thought of as surplus metal from their equipment – sometimes with disastrous consequences as the weakened components

In breaking the world hour record in 1984 Italian Francesco Moser upped the technological stakes by a considerable margin. From then on a plunging front-end, disc wheels but above all the aerodynamics of a bike were essential factors in machine design.

snapped well before the finishing line. The advent of the low profile design and the belief that lowering wind resistance was more important than saving weight brought an end to cutting and drilling.

Mike Burrows used his engineering skills to build his own low profile machine, but later he modified the design until he arrived at what he called 'the baby frame'. The sloping top tube was out; in its place was an almost conventionally-shaped frame, though much smaller than the average. It could be adapted to fit any size of rider by the use of longer seat posts and handlebar stems.

Burrows discarded the concept of the low profile bike in favour of an aerodynamic seat post, the seemingly innocuous component which attaches the seat to the frame of the bike. He believed that the forward motion of the rider created turbulence which could be most effectively dispersed by a teardrop shaped seat post. Cynics may have said that this was just another sales ploy: make the bike a bit different in order to sell a few more frames, but the development of the 'baby frame' is vital to the story of the Lotus bike, as it was this smaller, more compact shape which Burrows was to recreate in carbon fibre.

Burrows' father, Richard, was drafted into the project – his patternmaker's skills put to the task of making a 'wooden plug' in the shape the frame was to be. Mike then discussed with Mike Nelthorpe, an engineering colleague, the potential of using carbon fibre to build the frame. There was a minor problem, as Burrows explains: 'We'd never used carbon fibre before and we didn't even know where to get the stuff.' After much discussion they decided it would be suitable, and having found a supplier, stage two began.

Nelthorpe made a two-piece mould, putting a dividing line down the centre of the wooden plug. Then, using glass fibre, he took a mould of each side. Next they poured into the mould a polyurethane mix, which foamed up as it settled. The mix hardened into a solid foam frame shape, which was sanded down and wrapped in carbon fibre before being placed back into the mould. As it was now slightly oversized the carbon fibre was compressed onto the surface, which improved the quality of the finish. The carbon fibre-wrapped foam was left overnight to harden, and the next

day Mike Burrows had his first prototype Windcheetah frame. It was autumn 1984, and after a winter spent refining it, the bike made its first appearance in competition in May 1985.

Burrows used Windcheetah in a 10-mile time trial race: 'It was on May Day, which I thought was apt for a revolutionary bicycle.' Fellow competitors were not surprised by the bike, used as they were to seeing Burrows on unconventional machines. 'I did one of my fastest ever times that day. I had designed a faster bike, and no-one had done that for a hundred years'.

The euphoria did not last long. Burrows realized that others did not share his enthusiasm. A claim to have reinvented something which has been around for a century can expect to be met with scorn or indifference. For Mike Burrows, it was the latter, particularly from the people he had hoped to impress – the British cycle manufacturing industry. 'Nobody wanted to know. No-one could see its potential – or they couldn't see enough to want to invest in it. I felt like Einstein must have done, you know "look! $E=MC^2$ you fools, can't you see it?".' Disenchanted, but not completely disheartened, Burrows decided to show the bike to the Chief Executive of the British Cycling Federation (BCF). This time he had a better reception. 'Jim Hendry was the first official to recognize what it could mean, and he asked if the team could take it to Italy.'

In August 1985 Italy was the venue for the senior world championships. Hendry did not intend to use the bike in competition, but to show it to UCI officials there in order to gauge their reaction to the design. The officials promptly decided that the bike was not 'race legal' – but it was tried out in training by members of the British team. The British track squad that year included a 16 year-old junior rider, sent to the championships to gain experience after some impressive performances at home.

Chris Boardman could not have known as he circled the velodrome in Bassano that he was astride a prototype of the bike he would ride to Olympic victory in Barcelona, seven years hence. 'It was certainly an interesting concept, but I suppose with hindsight that prototype was crude compared to later models,' remembers Boardman of his first experience of a monocoque bike. The next time he would have any contact with Windcheetah would be in February 1992 when he was asked by Mike Burrows to take part in wind tunnel tests.

In the mid-1980's, while Burrows was attempting to generate interest in his bike there was quite separately a series of developments in bicycle equipment which had until that point remained pretty much the same design for many years. Many of these developments were aimed at improving the aerodynamic qualities of the bike and its rider.

Some had questionable benefits – brake levers were redesigned so that the operating cables were concealed beneath the handlebar tape. How much drag the 5mm wide cables produced in their overt form is difficult to quantify, but the brakes sold on their aesthetic, if not aerodynamic, value. However, there were more substantial developments in the aerodynamic field – not least the clothing. Wool/acrylic mix garments were discarded as Lycra made cyclists sleeker and more aerodynamic by using all-in-one shorts and jerseys known as 'skinsuits'.

Aerodynamically shaped cycling helmets also made their debut in the period; these were slow to catch on, due perhaps to their less-than-flattering effect on the rider's physique, but their streamlining worth has since been proven.

A major leap forward came in January 1984

British professional Steve Poulter riding a Kirk Precision during a mid-1980's event. The Kirk, made from magnesium, had an aerodynamic cross-section.

when the Italian, Francesco Moser, smashed the world hour record, which is considered the blue riband of all cycling records. Moser used disc wheels which had been developed for the attempt, and which were immediately recognized as having a distinct advantage over conventional spoked wheels. The discs create less turbulence due to their flat, smooth surface, which contrasts with the mass of turbulence – and therefore drag – created by spoked wheels.

Disc wheels were to a certain extent superseded by the tri-spoke wheel – and the bike used by Chris Boardman in Barcelona had a disc on the rear and tri-spoke front wheel.

The mid 1980s will be assessed by cycling

historians as a pivotal period in the technological development of cycling equipment. At the time when Mike Burrows was claiming to have reinvented the bicycle, a group of cyclists in America were testing an item of equipment which would revolutionize the riding position during high-intensity races such as time trials and track pursuit racing. Pete Penseyeres, a long-distance expert specializing in the 3,000-mile Race Across America, had asked Raleigh America to develop a handlebar system which would allow him a degree of comfort during the trans-continental race. Raleigh produced a clip-on attachment which would allow Penseyeres to lean his forearms on pads, his arms outstretched. It was only when triathletes adopted the clip-ons for the cycling sections of their competition that the aerodynamic potential of these comfort aids was recognized.

Generally, mainstream cyclists in the US and Europe ignored these handlebar developments and it was only when another, better-known, American began using them that they gained credibility. Greg LeMond used the tri-bars, as they are now known, during the time trial stages of the 1989 Tour de France. When he emerged the victor of that three-week long race by just eight seconds after winning the final time trial, racing cyclists at all levels began to look seriously at these aerodynamic aids.

I n the meantime, Mike Burrows was constantly evaluating the Windcheetah. In 1986 he visited Coventry's Transport Museum and while looking over a Victorian era 'Invincible' bicycle he saw something which was to become a key factor in the aerodynamic element of both his bicycle and later the LotusSport. The Invincible did not have the standard forks to hold the front wheel in place; instead there was a monoblade – a single

Boardman and Burrows with the Windcheetah machine. Note the early version of the monoblade fork, road gearing and conventional low-profile bars.

arm which enabled the tyre to be changed without removing the wheel. Its potential did not strike Burrows immediately: 'It was on the train on the way home. I realized that the single blade would look nice on my bike – and what's more it would be aerodynamic.' The monoblade was duly incorporated into Windcheetah. Mike had no way of knowing for certain that this monoblade – or indeed, the whole bike – had any aerodynamic qualities. He is an intuitive engineer and designer who worked from a series of ideas on how he thought wind resistance could be lowered.

In spite of the improvements, Windcheetah

was still deemed illegal for race use by the UCI. At the same time, British cycle manufacturers were still oblivious to any marketability of the bike. The combination of these factors meant that at the end of 1987 Burrows decided not to renew his design registration. There seemed to be no point. Industry didn't want the bike, and it couldn't be used in international competition.

The project was placed to one side while Mike continued with his other business interest – manufacturing coin packaging machines. On the sporting side, he increased his involvement in HPV. But Windcheetah was not forgotten. During 1989 and 1990 he made further improvements to its design, including the monoblade, which was now made from solid carbon fibre. A major turning point in the bike's story occurred in autumn 1990, when a rewording of Regulation 49 of the UCI guidelines on bicycle specification allowed a carbon fibre monocoque to be used in international competition. After eight years, Windcheetah was now race legal.

In 1991, with the project as far advanced as Burrows was able to take it, there took place one of those fateful occurrences that are essential to all good stories. Mike knew as an acquaintance a Belgian by the name of Rudi Thomann, whose work had brought him to England several years earlier. As well as being a keen amateur racing cyclist, Thomann had an avid interest in high-performance racing cars. Since his retirement as a Formula Two racing driver he had worked as a development engineer for the Lotus group at their Hethel factory, just outside Norwich.

Thomann and Burrows discussed Mike's frustrated attempts to launch Windcheetah. When he saw the sleek lines of the carbon fibre monocoque in Burrows' workshop, Thomann was impressed. He asked if he could take it to the Lotus factory to show it to other engineers. Burrows felt he had

nothing to lose, and agreed. The engineers were impressed. With less than 12 months to go before the Barcelona Olympic Games, an audacious plan began to develop. Thomann believed that Lotus could take the design further and that the bike could win the Olympic 4,000 metre pursuit race.

The name Lotus brings to mind fast sports cars. Emma Peel, the 1960's *Avengers* icon drove one. James Bond's amphibious car was a Lotus. Jim Clark, Colin Chapman and Lotus cars were a formidable team. Pedal cycles are certainly not the first things that spring to mind when the name of Lotus is mentioned.

Patrick Peal, the company's head of communications, explains why Lotus became involved. 'It was Rudi who said that this bike had many Lotus characteristics. It was fast, light, structurally interesting, very efficient and had few separate parts. It embodied everything Lotus is known for.' It may also be said that the lure of a potential Olympic gold medal could draw a company into a project; even a company facing the problems which Lotus had at that time. Olympic gold would give them a shop window to the world. The company had previously been involved in other non-motor racing schemes, namely boat building and microlight production. Whatever the reasons, Lotus saw what the British cycle manufacturing industry failed to see. A potential world beater and – perhaps more important – a potential market leader.

Thomann sold the idea to his employers. Despite some reservations they agreed to begin a development programme for the bike.

Mike Burrows was just glad that someone was prepared to invest in his dream. 'To their eternal credit, Lotus were the first people to recognize what I had done.' He was so grateful that in February 1992 he signed the design rights for his bicycle over to Lotus, and work began immediately.

The first stage was to ascertain just how aerodynamic the bike was. Lotus aerodynamicist, Richard Hill, began his involvement in the project – as did Chris Boardman, by this time Britain's fast-rising cycling star and, despite a failure at the 1991 world championships, still the home team's highest hope for Olympic success.

Speed and aerodynamics are even more vital in pursuit racing than in time trialling. A pursuit race is seen as the purest form of bike racing. It is rider matched against rider on opposite sides of a velodrome (the steeply banked timber cycle track). The bicycles have one single fixed gear, which means that you cannot freewheel. There are no brakes. To slow down, you ease back on the pedals. But in a pursuit race the rider has no interest in reducing speed. It is a high intensity race which lasts a little over four minutes, in which the competitors are in pursuit of each other. If one is caught the race is over immediately. If the race goes the full distance the winner is the rider who has closed the gap on his opponent. This is Chris Boardman's race. He was the best pursuiter in Britain – and he wanted the best bike to take to Barcelona. When Mike Burrows phoned to ask if he was interested in taking part in some tests with the bike being developed by Lotus, Boardman immediately agreed. There were now just six months to go before the Olympic Games.

To test how aerodynamic something is – be it a car, a boat or a bicycle – a wind tunnel is used. The subject is positioned in a jetstream of icy air. The further the air goes without breaking up, the less aerodynamic drag there is, which should result in the subject going faster. In this case, it was not only the bike being tested, but the rider too, and the reality of the test proved a shock for Chris Boardman. 'I had seen pictures of Greg LeMond in

a wind tunnel test, but it never occurred to me how cold it would be,' he recalls, adding that for the first test he was wearing nothing more than a Lycra skinsuit. 'The wind chill factor took the temperature down to about minus ten degrees Centigrade. After the first two tests I had to put more clothes on, which the aerodynamicist (watching from a separate room) wasn't too keen on, as it made me less aerodynamic.'

The first results from these sessions were not entirely encouraging. They indicated that Windcheetah was not cheating the wind at all. Richard Hill explains: 'It appeared that the bike was generating 6.6 percent more aerodynamic drag than Chris's conventional bike.'

It transpired that these disappointing figures were more to do with the position that Boardman was in than with the bike itself. The bike was not fitted with tri-bars and its standard handlebars were set for Mike Burrows, not Boardman. The problem was overcome by taping Chris's arms into a tri-bar position and lowering his upper body. Although Richard Hill is an acknowledged expert in car aerodynamics, he knew nothing about cycling. Yet, ironically, it was this lack of knowledge which gave the team their breakthrough. Hill kept asking Boardman if he could lower his position even further – something which a cyclist, bound by the conventions of what is and is not acceptable, would have been reticent to ask. Mike Burrows points out: 'A cyclist would never think of questioning the riding position of someone like Chris Boardman.' Crucially, Boardman could, and did, get his position lower. This made all the difference. Air now flowed freely between him and the bike, reducing the drag, and the next test results indicated that the bike would travel faster. There was another, natural, factor involved. Richard Hill told Chris that if he could have asked

Wind tunnel tests were inconclusive at first but it was soon discovered that Chris was unusually flexible for a cyclist and was able to ride lower and flatter than ever before. That, combined with the slippery profile of the Lotus, made for a formidable combination.

for a specific body shape he wouldn't have altered Chris's. 'My rounded back, which isn't exactly desirable in everyday life, turned out to be an aerodynamic advantage, maximized by the new low position.' In the final six months of his own intensive preparation, Boardman was now fully committed to a bike which he believed would help in his bid to win British cycling's first Olympic gold medal for 72 years.

Despite this good news, early 1992 was not the best of times for the Lotus group, as the internal wranglings of the company and the effects of the economic recession meant that 300 workers were laid off. Weekly car production was down to single figures, but by now the team were so committed that it was inconceivable that the project would not go ahead. Encouraged by Thomann, whose belief in the bike kept things moving during these difficult days, the production of the first LotusSport bike began in a portakabin in the company car park. Lotus decided to use carbon fibre, but their methods differed slightly from those used by Mike Burrows. The man who had devised the concept of this carbon fibre monocoque bike felt that he was not welcome when Lotus began building the frame. 'I wanted to see how they did the moulding – it would have been nice to learn a bit about what they were doing, but I didn't get to see it,' said Burrows, shortly after the Olympic Games.

Compare the upright position of Chris on a Merckx-style early 1970's track bike (top left) with the 1990's position where the forearms are parallel to the ground, the back much flatter and the knees are in front of the pedals.

Lotus began by using techniques more akin to dressmaking than engineering. A paper pattern for one side of the monocoque was laid on a length of carbon fibre, which was then cut out to the shape of the cycle frame. Two moulds were prepared for the carbon fibre cut-outs and the fabric was pressed into the corners. It was then plastered with a strong resin, binding the carbon fibres together and strengthening them. The direction of the fibre's weave was altered at the key pressure points of the frame to add more strength. It was then vacuum-baked at 80 degrees Centigrade, emerging after five hours as two hard, strong and light sides of a frame which were then bonded together. The

first Lotus monocoque frame was ready.

Although Mike Burrows claims that he was excluded from the development process, Lotus have different memories of events. Richard Hill explains that the company consulted Burrows at every stage of the bike's development up to Barcelona, adding: 'We utilized him as an engineering facility. Any advice he had to give we took on board, but if we didn't agree with it we didn't act on it.'

The first 'Lotus' was essentially the same as Burrows' Windcheetah. The team went back to the wind tunnel, and with tri-bars and Boardman's revised position, this time the test results were so good that those involved began to think not 'if' but 'when' Boardman and Lotus would win the gold. Barcelona and the 4,000 metre pursuit were now just three months away. While the first Lotus bike, Proto I, was being prepared for competition the company went ahead with further prototypes. Each of these was to differ in some way from the Burrows original.

As the gulf widened between the individuals involved so did the gap between the original Windcheetah and what was becoming a Lotus bike. Richard Hill said: 'We took Burrows' original concept and identified its strengths and weaknesses, and what we had to do to turn it into an Olympic machine, which it certainly was not at the time we saw it.' But the main reason Burrows' original bike did not perform well in wind tunnel tests was because it did not have aerodynamic tri-bars – a fact highlighted in a BBC *QED* documentary screened in 1993. Once tri-bars were fitted, combined with Boardman's ultra low position, the results improved dramatically without any structural change to the bike.

Before the bike could be used at Barcelona, the UCI rules demanded that an innovative bike such as this be used in international competition before appearing at a major event such as the Olympic Games. Proto I was used for this purpose. Bryan Steele, a young prospect on the Great Britain track squad, was asked to ride it, first of all at an open national track meeting at Leicester and later at Hyeres, the French venue for the World Cup series. At Hyeres the French team director, Daniel Morelon, was not impressed with what he saw. Doug Dailey, the British team manager in Barcelona, remembers Morelon actually saying 'We do not take this bike seriously.'

If the UCI officials at Hyeres concurred that the bike was within the regulations this would be the necessary approval for its use at Barcelona. They did, and so the green light was given for further prototypes. Dailey is surprisingly frank about the UCI ratification of the bike. 'In a way, we duped the world at Hyeres. We showed them a bike which looked like the Lotus, but the bike used at Barcelona was a refined version of this prototype.'

In the middle of July, in the week before the opening ceremony in Barcelona, Norfolk was hit by a heatwave, which caused problems for the team working on Proto III, the bike Boardman would use to win a gold medal. The process involving the plastic resin and the carbon fibre was affected by the rise in temperature, so the team switched to a night shift, when the cooler temperature would allow the composite to harden properly.

On the morning of Friday 24 July 1992, Proto III was completed. That afternoon, carrying the frame as hand luggage, Richard Hill flew out to Barcelona, where the Lotus was handed over to Rudi Thomann. The bike was assembled on the following day, and on Sunday Chris Boardman gave it its first trial run at the Olympic velodrome. On Monday he began his Olympic challenge in the qualifying round by riding faster over 4,000 metres than anybody had ever done before.

The world sat up and took notice, and within three days the names Boardman and Lotus had become synonymous – together they had combined to make Chris the fastest pursuiter in the world. But the reporters and television commentators who told this story seemed unaware of at least two critical human contributions: one of them given by the coach, Peter Keen, who guided and influenced Chris Boardman's career. Although Chris might agree with the suggestion that he could have won the Olympic pursuit title on a conventional bike, without Lotus, he is adamant on one point: 'Without Keen's help I would not have won the Olympic medal.'

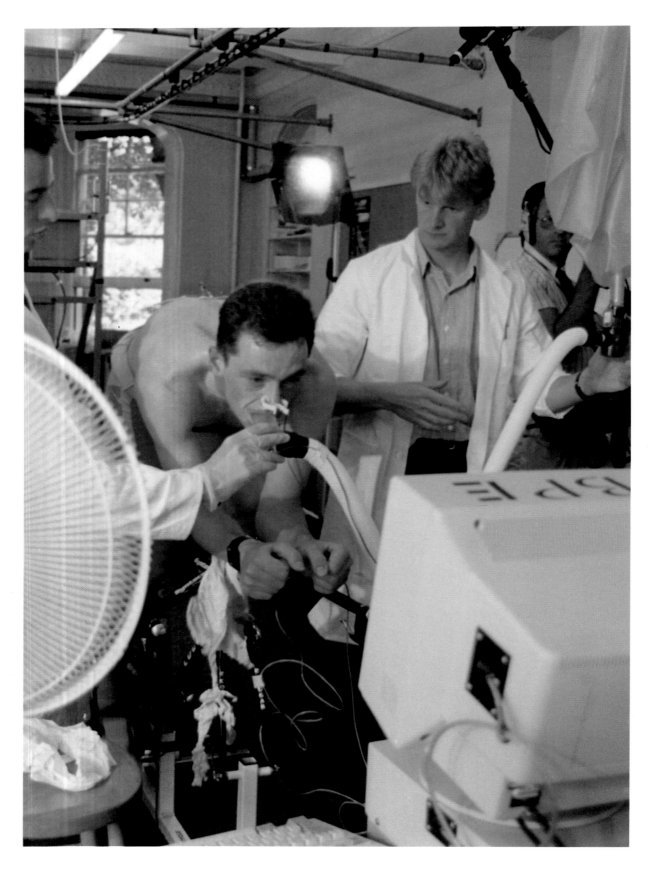

The Keen Edge

IF SOME OF THE MORE EXCITABLE TABLOID PRESS reports were to be believed, the Lotus bike was the secret of Boardman's success – end of story. Its photogenic and aerodynamic qualities certainly dazzled the media – so much so that it failed to focus on the human factors involved. These were the rider himself and the man who has been described by Doug Dailey, the British cycling team manager at Barcelona, as 'the most important contributory factor in the success story of Chris Boardman'.

He was talking about Peter Keen, the sports science lecturer and cycling coach without whose help Chris Boardman readily acknowledges that he would not have won the Olympic gold.

Peter Keen is more modest: 'I would say I am perhaps the second most important factor. The most important in the success of Chris Boardman is Chris himself.'

The close partnership of Boardman and Keen did not begin immediately after their first meeting in January 1987, but evolved gradually as they came into contact with each other through the British Cycling Federation's new attitude to a more scientific approach to preparation and training.

The first tests that Peter carried out on the 18 year-old hope of British cycling in Chichester were not promising. 'He was a little overweight after a winter of mainly running and gym

ABOVE: *Keen and the controversial Kingcycle used to measure Chris's steady improvements in power and endurance. Traditionalists felt that the tests were crude and often misleading as they were incapable of showing abstracts like 'drive' and 'character'.*

OPPOSITE: *Wired up – Boardman's breathing is monitored by Peter Keen at a test session in Keen's Chichester laboratory.*

work, and had let himself go a bit. He hadn't done much cycling, and I was certainly fitter than he was at that point.' The tests were to gauge Chris's current level of fitness, rather than how good he was. Peter Keen knew the potential of his subject, but felt there was more to come from him. He told Chris what he should be doing in training, and that he should return in three months' time.

As a racing cyclist himself, Peter Keen had questioned the established ideas regarding training for top level cycle racing. He believed that some of the old ideas were not based on any clear understanding of what the riders were trying to achieve, and that a lot of time spent 'training' was wasted. Peter devised his own training programme (described in detail later in this chapter) based on the premise that each time the rider trained on his bike an improvement in the rider's performance would

Chris takes his warm-down bike from mechanic Sandy Gilchrist after a pursuit round at the 1986 world championships in Colorado, USA. These were learning years for Boardman and he often found himself up against older and stronger opponents at international level.

be gained, and fitness would be achieved by careful planning. These ideas formed the basis of Boardman's training after that first meeting. He went back to see Keen in April. 'By that time he'd made a staggering improvement. He was now the sort of athlete I would have expected to see in January,' says Keen, impressed by both the rapidity of the improvement and by Boardman's willingness to listen to and learn new ideas. 'He was shocked into action by the January results, and shocked into listening by what happened in the subsequent three months when he made the improvement'.

During these early sessions, Peter Keen made an assessment of Chris that he is happy to admit was inaccurate. Keen believed that if a rider was to develop into a world class pursuiter he must be of a size sufficient to produce power outputs of a high level, and it was from this perspective that Keen told the 5' 8", 10 stone cyclist he would not make a

pursuit rider. Pursuit riders were big, powerful individuals; men like Hugh Porter, Tony Doyle and Colin Sturgess. Sturgess and Doyle were also ten seconds faster over 4,000 metres than Chris Boardman. 'It was difficult to see how Chris was going to make the developments that at that time we thought were necessary to be a pursuiter', says Keen. Chris was undeterred by this initial forecast. His drive and ambition, combined with Keen's subsequent rethinking of the qualities of a pursuiter and the approach to training for this race, meant that physical size would no longer be a dominating factor.

Sports science is an area which is developing rapidly, and Keen is frank about his initial assessment of Boardman. 'The bottom line is, I know more now than I knew then. I don't claim to have all the answers – you just keep learning'. Chris was duly impressed by Keen's scientific approach to race training: 'Peter could explain why I was doing what I was doing, and that was what I liked.' While Chris may have followed his former mentor Eddie Soens unquestioningly, now with Peter Keen he was beginning to ask questions. 'He'd say, "let's think about it, present me with an argument, and if it's reasonable, let's do it",' recalls Keen.

Chris's first full season as a senior rider began in 1987, and his third place behind Colin Sturgess in the British pursuit championship was the beginning of another gradual progression which would eventually see him winning that title. In August he flew to Vienna to take part in his third senior championships where he wore British colours in two track events: the team pursuit and the individual kilometre time trial race in which he finished 26th.

THE HEART OF THE MATTER – MEASURING BOARDMAN'S PERFORMANCE

There is nothing mysterious about pulse rate monitoring – for decades athletes have gauged their state of fitness, or ill-health, by taking their resting heart rate from the number of beats they can feel in their pulse at the wrist or neck. But the advent of electronic transmitters, which were strapped around the chest and sent a constant heart rate reading to a wrist watch or computer screen, enabled athletes and trainers to chart the upper reaches of performance and thus develop training programmes tailored to an individual's heart rate profile. With a heart rate monitor Peter Keen could map out Chris's training and racing performances in incredible detail, and extract vital data to determine the effectiveness of his schedules – the target pace plans for each race.

120-MILE ROAD RACE

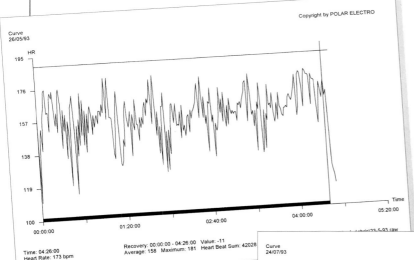

LEFT: *Chris's pulse chart for the 1993 Manchester GP shows the constant changes of pace in a road race. The regularly spaced peaks indicate a hill which was covered several times in this circuit race and the final flurry of effort shows Chris's battle with Brian Smith, who scored a rare victory over the Wirral man. Note the figures at the bottom which show a relatively unstressful average heartbeat of 158 BPM and the maximum of 181 BPM.*

RIGHT: *There can be no mistaking Chris's extraordinary profile for his successful hour record ride in Bordeaux, France, in 1993. Boardman is a masterly judge of pace and this reading is an excellent example of his ability to reach a level and then hold it for one hour. Look at the average – 183 beats per minute (BPM) is very high compared to his maximum of 193 BPM which was reached at the end when Chris threw everything into his finish and the terrible humidity in the stadium took its toll.*

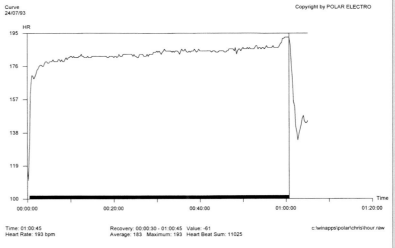

THE HOUR RECORD

Chris (at the bottom of the track) takes part in a team pursuit training session at Leicester prior to the Seoul Olympics in 1988. Boardman was a regular member of the GB team pursuit squad during the latter part of the 1980s and early 1990s.

After Vienna, Chris began his preparation for 1988 and the Seoul Olympics. Just before leaving for South Korea he raced to second place in the British pursuit championships, again behind Colin Sturgess. Boardman's first Olympics gave him valuable insights into the scale and pressure of such a global event, but his result – 13th in the team pursuit – was not enough to satisfy him. The Olympic ideal, conceived by Baron Pierre de Coubertin, was no comfort. 'It doesn't appeal to me. I understand what it means about taking part being more important than winning, but the reality is very different.' Like all young people who compete at a high level Chris Boardman had dreams and ambitions. He wanted to be world and Olympic champion, and it was those goals that he strived for in his early years. But there were periods when he doubted his ability to reach those heights.

'At times I would think I couldn't do it, and I would scale it down a bit. I began thinking that a Commonwealth gold would be enough.'

In October he and Sally were married, and the 20 year-old had another set of responsibilities. They bought a house in Birkenhead, and in between decorating and looking for a job in his trade as a cabinet-maker, they became parents. Their son was named Edward after Eddie Soens, the man whose memory still inspired Chris. Meanwhile Chris prepared for the 1989 season, under the guidance of Peter Keen. The BCF appeared to be pleased with Keen's methods as it appointed him national track coach in 1989, at the age of 24.

Colin Sturgess had turned professional at the end of 1988 and Chris won the British amateur pursuit title for the first time the following year, just a month after winning his first senior British 25-mile championship. In all he won six British championships in 1989, but did not restrict himself to time trials and track racing. In May he took third place in the prestigious Tour of Lancashire, a four-day pro-am race – one of several impressive road race results which bore witness to Boardman's increasing versatility.

The world championships, held in France that August, gave him encouragement, with 10th place in the pursuit. The first and second-placed riders were representing countries which no longer exist, as Viatcheslav Ekimov wore the colours of the Soviet Union, while silver medallist Jens Lehmann was riding for East Germany. Riders from Iron Curtain countries had dominated world-class pursuit racing since 1981. (The only exception was at Los Angeles in 1984, when the Communist bloc boycotted the Olympic Games.) The subsequent collapse of Communism, and disarray in state-aided sporting centres of excellence, led many to believe that this would mean an end to Eastern-bloc dominance in cycle racing.

The progress in Chris's pursuiting career continued, with third place in the team pursuit event at the Commonwealth Games held in Auckland, New Zealand, in February 1990. From the warmth of New Zealand, home to the English cold and Chris began his racing season with the usual mix of time trials and medium distance road races which he used as basic preparation for the national and world championships in the summer months.

But as the season progressed he became aware of stomach pains which became more intense by the week. Doctors could find no obvious reason, but the pain persisted. 'It was absolute agony. When the attacks came I was doubled up with pain.' He was taken into hospital, where doctors, unable to find a cause, gave injections of dimorphine, a pain killer. 'As soon as each attack passed I felt better, so I could live with it.' In between these attacks his racing continued, although he was concerned about the cause of the problem.

By now it was June and the national 25-mile title had to be defended, over a course on the outskirts of Hull. The Friday before the race, just as they were about to leave, Chris suffered another attack. Sally drove to the east coast with Chris lying in the back of the car, holding on to a bucket in case he was sick. 'I can't believe we did it, looking back. I think it was because Sally had booked the accommodation and didn't want to cancel it!'.

Sally has a different view. 'I knew that once he got there he'd be alright, so I insisted that we went.' As the doctors hadn't been able to identify the

cause, Sally thought it may have been nothing more than a bad attack of pre-race nerves, something which had troubled the early part of his career.

The pain did not abate and they went straight to Hull City Infirmary, where Chris was treated until the early hours of Saturday, the day before the race. 'I didn't feel too bad the next morning; I went for a ride round the course and decided to race.' He won the championship, but two days later was taken into hospital. The apparently healthy appendix, subject of much examination, was a decoy. A routine 20-minute operation turned into a five-and-a-half-hour marathon as it was discovered that

Germany's Jens Lehmann was the revelation of the 1991 world championship pursuit series. His times, some nine seconds faster than Boardman's best were helped by a carbon fibre machine developed specifically for the series.

he had a twisted bowel – a condition that Peter Keen believes may have been responsible for the dips in form that Chris suffered in the years up to 1990, when he was sometimes unable to recover quickly from strenuous effort. Chris duly obeyed his doctor's orders to rest following the operation, riding his bike – gently – for a couple of weeks. In August 1990 he had another title to defend – the pursuit championship won for the first time the year before – at the British Track Championships at Leicester.

He had decided not to race in the championship because of the operation and the lack of training. He thought that he wouldn't have the necessary form, but the night before the championship opened, Chris raced in a 10-mile time trial and finished with the fastest time, 20 minutes, 35 seconds. This was all the encouragement he needed. 'Sally and I just packed for the week and drove to Leicester the next morning.' Chris took the silver medal behind Simon Lillistone, enough to impress Great Britain team manager Doug Dailey, who told him he had been selected for the team for the world championships to be held at Maebashi, Japan.

Just eight weeks after major abdominal surgery, Chris Boardman recorded his fastest time yet in a 4,000 metre pursuit race, improving by 12 seconds to finish with 4 minutes, 36 seconds, and eventually seventh place in the world championship. Although he was four seconds behind the winner, Evgenii Berzin of the USSR, it was the phenomenal improvement from his previous fastest time, which convinced him and Peter Keen that he could win the world championship pursuit race.

The unfocused aims of the past four years were now replaced by an absolute clarity of purpose. Keen sees this post-operation period as the 'freeing' of Boardman: 'Underneath this problem there was an extremely fit athlete just waiting to burst out.'

Tenth place in the 1989 world pursuit championship in France was encouraging for Chris. The winner that year was Estonian Viatcheslav Ekimov who later turned professional and recorded some notable successes.

The closer involvement with Keen meant that Boardman had changed his training methods from the well-established ideas – essentially long hours in the saddle 'getting the miles in' – to a new approach devised by Keen which could be described as 'sacrificing quantity for quality'.

The old training methods were based on the macho assumption that it was essential to 'toughen up' the individual. Every day would be spent training in some way: Saturday and Sunday would be racing days, Monday a rest day – which meant typically a 20- to 40-mile ride – Tuesday and Thursday 30 to 50 miles on the 'chain gang' (a quasi-race in which 10 to 20 riders constantly relay each other to the front of the pack in order to push the pace higher and higher). Wednesday would entail at least 100 miles, again in a group, and Friday would be repeat of Monday. The quality of such training was assessed simply in terms of mileage achieved each week. This was how it had always been. It appeared to have worked for decades, so why question it?

Peter Keen did question it. He reasoned that such a training method was not based on a clear understanding of the way in which training actually improves athletic performance. In his view, six hours of cycling does not always mean six hours of effective training, especially if the pace is not high enough to achieve what Keen describes as a positive training effect – where the body modifies itself in order to cope better with the stresses of intense exercise. By recording heart rates of riders during the long group rides he discovered that rarely more than two out of five or more were spent at an effective training intensity, the remaining hours were simply consuming valuable recovery time. Rest and recovery was largely ignored by traditional racing cyclists, who believed that a day off training would result in a dramatic drop of fitness. In reality such constant, uninterrupted training often results in a state of chronic fatigue, a condition that prevents many riders reaching their true potential during competition.

Keen devises training programmes that try to ensure that each time a rider trains, he or she will gain a positive training effect. He argues the idea is not as radical as many believe. It is simply a blending of sound physiological knowledge, common sense and experience gained from listening to feedback. Keen has no doubt that the old system created 'tough cyclists' capable of tolerating fatigue and discomfort but argues 'that may be the best way to train a paratrooper, but it's not what an elite athlete needs.'

At the heart of Keen's training philosophy is the division of physical effort in to four levels of intensity ranging from very light exercise causing little or no stress (level 1) up to a flat-out effort that will cause exhaustion in a matter of seconds or minutes (level 4). Each is defined and controlled by measuring heart rate, and in Chris's case a number of other physiological responses measured in a laboratory. Level 2 efforts lasting one to four hours form the core of Keen's training programmes, as at this intensity substantial training effects are achieved without having to expose riders to the more physiologically demanding level 3 and 4 efforts. These are reserved for specialized training and only account for 20 percent of the total training load. Level 3 sessions are the equivalent of riding 10- to 25-mile time trial, so many races are often viewed as training. Level four workouts are performed above race pace, so efforts have to be interspersed with sufficient rest to enable recovery – the classic interval training system so often used by runners and swimmers.

Keen's training programmes are therefore a complex blend of work-outs with differing intensities and duration, each tailored to the individual need of the cyclist, and always aimed at maximizing the training effect. The mileage at the end of the week was no longer of importance. He thus kept the good points from the old system, but abandoned its damaging overtraining effects.

Encouraged by his performance in the world championships, and using Keen's methods, Chris began his preparation for Stuttgart in 1991. The German city was the venue for the world championships, and in February Chris, Peter and team manager Doug Dailey met to agree a strategy. 'We planned how we were going to win the world championship pursuit race,' says Keen. 'It's a terribly

By 1992 Chris was the undisputed star of British time trialling and a record time for 25 miles of 47minutes, 19 seconds was a big improvement on the old figures. It was even more impressive when he later revealed that he was unable to put his bike in top gear.

difficult psychological threshold to cross, to actually say "we are going to win it" ', but it had to be done.' Up until June, that plan would go according to schedule.

In 1991 Chris Boardman effectively 'arrived' on the British racing scene, at least as far as the mainstream cycling press was concerned. His victory in a hotly-contested 'hilly' 25-mile race early in the season seemed to come as a surprise to one cycling magazine, whose reporter lamented the fact that 'he is not as well known as he should be'. Some of

Chris's supporters pointed out that if cycling journalists had been doing their job effectively and taken into account his 14 national championship victories between 1985 and 1990, then perhaps he would have been more widely known. This soon became irrelevant as within months the name of Chris Boardman became familiar to just about every cyclist in the country.

Be it time trials or road races, Chris was winning virtually every weekend, including his first major stage race, the four-day Tour of Lancashire. This is a tough pro-am race in which he had previously finished third in 1989. It is held over the uncompromising roads around the Trough of Bowland, and the professionals were keen to win. With little team support and against a united professional class, Boardman's victory was a classic one as the amateur rider took on and broke the professional teams who were out to prevent him winning. In all the races he finished in the UK in 1991, he lost only three. Says Chris: 'For the first time in my career I was training as effectively as I could. I was on top of it all the time, just cruising along.'

As well as the Tour of Lancashire victory he won seven national championships in 1991, including the track pursuit title and the 25- and 50-mile championships.

Everything Chris Boardman did in this year was designed to bring him to peak fitness in late August for the world championship pursuit race. Back in 1990 he had been just four seconds off Berzin's winning time and, encouraged by his successes during 1991, he re-evaluated his original aims for Stuttgart. 'It's funny how you alter things as you go along. At first I thought I wanted a medal. As it got closer I realized that nothing but the gold would do.'

His confidence was boosted when he broke the amateur world record for 5,000 metres at Leicester, two weeks before the world championship. His time of 5 minutes, 47.70 seconds was 2.5 seconds faster than the previous holder, Denmark's Hans Henrik Oersted, who set his figures at altitude in Mexico City in 1979.

In Stuttgart, the world championship series started promisingly, and in the qualifying round Boardman did 4 minutes, 31 seconds – five seconds faster than the previous year in Japan. There, he had finished seventh, one place in front of the German, Jens Lehmann. Now, in front of his home crowd, Lehmann produced, out of nowhere, a ride of 4 minutes, 22 seconds on his way to winning the gold medal Boardman had hoped for. Chris could not improve on his qualifying time and finished 9th, a result which left him devastated. 'I'd clawed

my way there, and the goal posts had been moved.'

Chris felt that nine seconds was an insurmountable gap in pursuit racing. 'I thought about packing it in and spent the rest of the week looking for the highest balcony,' he says. Doug Dailey remembers Boardman's disappointment: 'I really thought that was the end of pursuiting for Chris. He took it very badly.'

Peter Keen shared Chris's disappointment. 'I thought "what do we do now?". After all that work it was a terrible blow.' But in the following weeks they began to analyze this setback. Keen believed that, despite the improvement in his time, Chris wasn't at his best when he arrived for the Stuttgart championship. He pinpointed a time three months earlier as the cause. In June, when Chris won the British 50-mile title, he was suffering from the tail end of a viral infection which affected him for the next five or six months. 'He struggled all the time after the "50". He was never on top of the programme – never really buzzing.'

Chris Boardman had suffered setbacks in his

National coach Doug Dailey (below left) seen here with Chris, was a former international amateur racer and strong advocate of Keen's training regime for Chris .

The strain shows: Chris can't hide his exhaustion after a particularly strenuous training session, while Peter Keen analyzes the data printouts as part of his training method.

career before. He was twice beaten for the junior 25-mile championship and Colin Sturgess had been his *bête noire* in the junior and senior pursuit race. Chris had learned to handle these disappointments, and he and Peter still believed that he could win the world championship. By November 1991 the confidence had begun to return to the partnership. They knew that their plan had worked well until June, and encouraged by this, they began planning for the next year – Olympic year. When the Olympic Games are held, there is no amateur pursuit world championship; it is in effect combined with the Olympic title, so it was with this in mind that their plans were made. Once more they told themselves they could do it – but instead

of 'world champion', they were aiming at 'Olympic champion'.

'We knew that with some adjustments to the training programme we could win a medal in Barcelona,' says Chris. The adjustments were based on information they had on Jens Lehmann, the world champion at Stuttgart. Using his winning time and physiological details, Keen was able to compute the power that Lehmann was generating. He then calculated the power Chris would need to beat him. They now had a target – and ten months to close the gap.

At the same time as Keen and Boardman discussed their Olympic plans, designer Mike Burrows and Lotus were talking about the bike they believed could win a medal at Barcelona. It couldn't win on its own – it would need a rider capable of racing at the most competitive level – and Burrows believed Boardman could be that rider. The timing of the phone call from Mike Burrows to Chris, asking whether the racer would like to become involved with Lotus, was perfect. It slotted neatly into Boardman's and Keen's plan. The possibility of using the Lotus bike would, if for no other reason, give a psychological boost to Chris in his quest for a gold medal.

The Olympic year of 1992 did not start ideally for Chris. He was troubled with illness and injury in the early part of the season's build up. As the season progressed, Chris divided his time between his family (Edward now had a sister, Harriet), his racing and training, and tests with the embryonic Lotus bike. The tests and subsequent negotiations involved frequent 12-hour round trips between Hoylake and Norwich, which took up precious training and recuperation time.

But in early June the results started to come: Chris set a new British record for 25 miles in early June, with 47 minutes, 19 seconds. Seven days later his fourth consecutive win in the British 25-mile championship confirmed that his training schedule was on target for Barcelona, now just six weeks away.

As well as racing and training there were regular tests on a Kingcycle rig to gauge the power output that Chris was able to generate. The Kingcycle is a static machine that allows the rider to connect their own bike to a computer in order to take a subjective measure of the rider's relative power. These tests are carried out over a period of time in order to monitor the rider's progress.

Less than a month before the Olympic Games started Chris was due to be tested at Peter Keen's laboratory in Chichester. Team manager Doug Dailey didn't want Chris to make the long journey south and suggested Keen travelled up to his farm-house in North Wales, where he had a Kingcycle set up. The test underway, Dailey went into the kitchen of his home to make some coffee for Keen: 'While I was there, Peter came in and said "The gold medal is on!"' The realization that Chris could win it began to sink in. The Kingcycle results showed that Chris Boardman had exceeded the power values that Keen believed were necessary to close the gap on Lehmann. There were now four weeks until the opening ceremony of the Olympic Games.

Chris was getting fully psyched up: 'I was really fresh, I'd just got to a peak – a level I hadn't reached for a long time.' This was quite a different story to his build up for Stuttgart, arriving (as he now knew) jaded from the after-effects of a virus.

The first training sessions at Barcelona's Horta velodrome underlined this new fitness. Using the track in quiet moments, away from the watchful eyes of his rivals and their trainers, he recorded times which made it clear that he was a contender for the top honours. One of these practices was witnessed by Charlie Walsh, the manager of the Australian team, who couldn't believe his stop-watch. Chris did 3 minutes, 18 seconds for three kilometres. Another kilometre (to make the total race distance) at this pace would have given him 4 minutes, 22 seconds: enough to let everyone know that he was on top form.

In Chris's training diary after this session there is written one word: 'Pleased'. Word began to filter around the Olympic Village that the Briton was going to do something special.

Doug Dailey knew that Chris Boardman could win the pursuit title, but was concerned about the media pressures that this would bring. As a former Olympian, Dailey had seen the press machine in action.and he was worried that if Chris looked set for a place in the final, the media attention would distract him. He needed to convince the British

Olympic Association, the organization looking after all British athletes' interests at Barcelona, that they needed to protect Chris. He told the BOA, who were initially sceptical, that Boardman was out for a medal – probably the gold. 'I said that something dramatic was going to happen at the velodrome. I knew that we couldn't handle the press when it did'.

Dailey had made an accurate assessment. Following Chris's qualifying ride, when he recorded an Olympic record time of 4 minutes, 27.357 seconds, not only the medal-hungry British press, but the world's media representatives descended on the velodrome. Dailey managed to convince the BOA, and they placed people there to protect Chris from the journalists' efforts to get an angle on 'The young Briton and his amazing superbike'.

Monday, 27 July 1994 – the opening day of the Olympic competition – began at 9:00am for Chris Boardman. Along with the rest of the British team he had a half-hour ride around the roads of the Olympic Village before heading back to his room for a sleep. Lunch was at three in the afternoon and mealtimes were re-scheduled because the races were to be held in the evening. Once at the Horta velodrome Chris warmed up for 20 minutes, using his road bike on static rollers, before lining up for the first of four rounds – the qualifying round, second round, semi-finals and the final – which would total around 17 minutes of the hardest racing in order to clinch the gold medal.

By definition, a pursuit race involves two riders each pursuing the other from opposite sides of the same track – effectively half a lap's distance. A lap time can vary from 18 to 22 seconds – depending on the velodrome. In the qualifying rounds, which are run as a series of pursuit races, the rider

has to achieve as fast a time as possible, to decide the seeding for the following rounds. As the series progresses, the fastest rider always meets the slowest, which keeps the top riders apart until the final rounds.

Despite breaking the Olympic record at the early qualifying stage in the competition, Chris was not happy since he expected Jens Lehmann to go faster. The German started off well, his time better than Chris's after four laps, but from this point he began slipping behind. Lehmann finished with a time of 4 minutes, 30.054 seconds. Lehmann knew the size of his task, as to close a three-second gap is considered virtually impossible in pursuit racing.

Chris Boardman always appears calm and collected, but after the Monday qualifying round the realization of what he was about to do sent him into what he describes as a series of panic attacks. The BCF had engaged a psychologist, John Syers, for the Games and sessions with John helped Chris deal with the emotions he was feeling. There were other ways that the Olympic champion-to-be eased the pressure. 'I went to the cinema in the Olympic Village. It was air conditioned, so it was really cool and dark – very relaxing.' Chris watched The Commitments, the lighthearted film helping to take his mind off his own commitment… at least for a time. 'While I was there I became totally submerged in the film. Then I would realize with a start where I was, what I was there for, and start panicking again.'

The press reaction that Dailey had forecast was making itself felt back in the UK too. Immediately after the qualifying round, Keith and Carol Boardman found their lives disrupted by the arrival on their doorstep of the media newshounds. When it became clear that Chris was the favourite, one British tabloid newspaper offered to fly Keith, Carol and the children out to

Barcelona – an offer they refused.

Some members of the press chose a different angle with Doug Dailey. 'It was amazing. I've never seen press attention like it in my life. We were threatened and intimidated. One guy from a tabloid paper told me that they could make or break Chris Boardman, and it wouldn't be in his interests if we turned down an exclusive interview.' Dailey chose to ignore any chequebook or strong arm journalistic tactics and Chris remained protected in the Olympic Village.

The second round (quarter-finals) took place on Tuesday evening. Once again Boardman set another Olympic record with 4 minutes, 24.496 seconds, on his way to catching his opponent, Jan-Bo Petersen of Denmark, who had knocked Chris out of the competition at this stage 12 months earlier in Stuttgart. Chris caught Petersen with five laps remaining. On the last lap he eased up: 'I knew it was a good time, but I wanted to let them see I had eased off, so I sat up and put my hands on top of the bars.' He wasn't taking anything for granted, but this round gave him confidence: 'I think I realized I could win it after this.'

Lehmann was a beaten man before Wednesday's final, demoralized by Boardman's second-round time and the fact that he had cruised the last lap. It wasn't the bike that Boardman was riding that psyched the German out – it was the times he was recording and the apparent ease with which Boardman caught his opponents.

As the news broke that Chris's qualifying round was no fluke, a cycling cynic back in Wirral was overheard to say that he would eat his hat if Boardman did anything in Barcelona. This kind of cynicism was not entirely unfounded. Year after year British teams had travelled to world and Olympic championships with high hopes, only to return empty-handed. This was new territory for cycling fans too, and many watching at home hardly dared believe Boardman could do it.

The Horta velodrome in Barcelona – the dramatic venue for Chris's triumph which was packed with fans, press and an enthusiastic crowd on the night of the 4,000 metre individual pursuit final.

Chris's father, Keith, arrived home from work on Tuesday, the night before the final, to see a group of 20 or more journalists outside his front gate, so decided to go to Chris's house instead. He was just about to let himself in when he heard a shout of 'There he is!', as two cars disgorged their journalist occupants. 'I jumped back into my van, took off up the street and managed to lose them in the traffic. They congratulated me later on that!' The reason for his reticence was simply that neither he nor Carol were willing to tempt fate before the final was over by commenting on Chris's chances.

Sally had last seen Chris the week before the Games opened. She knew he was capable of winning the title, but it was only after the qualifying round that she realized that the dream was about to become reality. She had spent the previous weekend wondering whether or not to go to Barcelona, but now she was decided. After the qualifying round, Chris had phoned her to ask if she'd seen the race on television. 'He said he'd phone me the following night, but I told him not to – I think he guessed then that I'd fly out.'

Sally had noticed an advert in a magazine offering accommodation in Barcelona. Convinced it would be taken, she took a chance and phoned the number. The woman who answered had just been watching Chris on television, and was amazed to receive a phone call from the wife of the Olympic contender. Arrangements were made for Sally to stay, and she flew out on Tuesday morning. That afternoon, looking for the velodrome and unable to speak Spanish, she searched for someone 'who looked English', to ask directions. Eventually spotting one, she asked him if he knew where the cycle track was. 'He asked me if I was going to see this young Boardman. I said, "yes, I'm his wife".' Of all the people to choose from, Sally had just told a British reporter that she was the wife of their most

wanted man. She was soon surrounded by journalists and photographers, but once they had taken some pictures and extracted some quotes they directed her to the velodrome.

Sally didn't have a ticket so she bought one at double the price from a tout outside the stadium. By chance she found herself with a trackside seat – the best location for watching the second round, and the following day's semi-final and final.

After the second round Sally went to meet Chris, but because she was suffering from a virus and didn't want to pass it on to her husband, they spoke to each other across a room for a few minutes, before Chris was whisked off to the Olympic Village.

On Tuesday night, with less than 20 hours to go before he would have to ride the semi-final and the final, Chris managed to get to sleep by mentally designing the perfect racing bike – a method he often uses when sleep eludes him. 'I lie there and think what I would use and how I would have this piece of equipment – stuff like that. I soon drift off that way…'.

Chris was up by nine o'clock on Wednesday, and went through the by now usual routine of a short ride, a sleep and lunch. By lunchtime the pressure was beginning to affect him. 'It was like a dream. I could see everyone around me talking, eating, laughing – but it was as though I wasn't a part of it. People were talking to me but I couldn't hold a proper conversation.' He hadn't come this far to let his nerves destroy his Olympic dream.

As the final drew nearer he became focused on what he had to do, nervousness suppressed until the starter's gun would convert that emotion into energy. There was one more obstacle before Boardman could claim his place in the final. The semi-final round pitched him against Australia's Mark Kingsland, a man tipped for gold by many,

Chris and Sally embrace as the world looks on after the 1992 Olympic pursuit final. The following day some British newspapers used this image as their lead picture.

while Jens Lehmann would have to dispose of New Zealander Gary Anderson, before he could claim his place in the final.

The semi-finals – four and a half minutes of intense effort – would secure a place in the final, less than two hours later. The Lehmann-Anderson round took place first, and with the German emerging the winner, Boardman knew that he would face the reigning world pursuit champion if he could beat Kingsland. The semi-final underway, Chris was ahead at the first kilometre, and kept his lead over the Australian to finish with 4 minutes,

29.332 seconds – his slowest ride of the competition. Lehmann, on the other hand, had finished his semi-final in his fastest time of the series, 4 minutes, 27.230 seconds, which worried Chris as he prepared himself for the final, now just one hour away: 'I started thinking that perhaps Jens had been holding back through the other rounds, saving it all for the final,' says Chris. 'I felt a lot better when I saw him warming up. Jens was rubbing his legs, so I thought they must be giving him some pain.'

Sally had left the children, Edward and Harriet, with Chris's parents. On Wednesday night, just before the final, Keith and Carol were unable to settle at home, because of the crowds of reporters outside the door. They decided to go to Chris and Sally's house, but were followed. 'We sneaked into the back yard and climbed over the wall, passing the kids over,' says Carol. As Hoylake is full of back alleys and side streets, this helped in their escape. 'We took all the back routes, where the cars couldn't follow us, and went to my Mum's house.'

The newshounds had been given the slip, for the moment at least. Carol and her mother Olive, along with Edward and Harriet, sat down to watch the final of the Olympic pursuit championship. This family gathering were watching Chris as son, grandson and father on their television screen, with the most important four and a half minutes of his life in front of him. Keith was not there. Unable to bear watching the race on live television, he made a drink and went for a bath.

In the Horta velodrome at Barcelona, Chris went through the last few minutes of his preparation. Ten years of racing, training and constantly striving to 'be the best' was about to receive the ultimate test. A gentle warm-up on the rollers, and then it was time to sit astride the Lotus in the starting gate, the electronically-operated system which holds rider and machine until the starter's gun

releases the mechanism.

Lehmann, as the fastest rider from the previous round, started in the home straight. On the opposite side of the track Boardman battled with the same nervousness he had experienced at Stuttgart only 12 months previously. But he was now used to this feeling and able to deal with it: this time he knew he was a real contender for gold and certainly silver.

Nevertheless the pressures on Chris at this moment were tremendous. 'I couldn't look at the crowd – I didn't want to take the scale of it in, so I just looked at the track directly in front of me.' Glancing across the track just once at Lehmann, he prepared to make his effort at the signal. The starting gate jammed (as it had done in the second round) and a false start was called. This had happened to Chris many times during his international career, so his composure remained intact. 'I just wanted to get it over with. It had been dragging on for three days, and I was telling myself that it was just another four and a half minutes, and it would all be over.'

The second time there were no further problems and Boardman moved smoothly away from the gate. In a pursuit race the riders can check each other's progress by glancing across the track and Chris was keeping one eye on Lehmann. Chris was fractionally in the lead after one lap – 0.307 seconds – but by the time he and the German had covered one kilometre this lead had risen to just over one second. This may not sound much, but in the pursuit race a lead of two seconds can become

Chris, his face half covered by a specially made carbon fibre aero helmet, speeds through the Barcelona night air on his way to Britain's first gold medal of the 1992 Olympic Games. Note the monoblade fork, aerodynamic chainset and a Chris favourite – no socks.

55

unassailable, and three seconds becomes an insurmountable gap – beyond argument.

Three laps later Chris was nearly three seconds in front of the man who had destroyed his world championship dream a year before. He kept the pressure on; his upper body steady, his legs whirling that single fixed gear as he closed the half-lap distance between himself and Lehmann. In the pursuit, if a rider is caught by his opponent the race is immediately over. But at the Olympic Games this had never happened.

Back in Hoylake, sitting in his mother-in-law's bath with only a cup of tea and a sponge for company, Keith misinterpreted the noise from downstairs and feared the worst. 'I heard Carol screaming "He's catching him, he's catching him!" and I thought, "Oh no!". I thought Lehmann was catching Chris.'

There was no need to worry. Before they passed the 3,000 metre mark the 1991 world champion knew he was beaten. He had been floundering over the last four laps, his upper body rocking and his style unsmooth in contrast to the relentless rhythm and pace rapped out by his pursuer. As the electronic clock read 4 minutes 10 seconds, Chris Boardman overtook Lehmann as they swung off the banking onto the back straight. It was all over. Boardman raised his right arm in the air. He was Olympic champion, the first in the history of the Olympic pursuit final to catch his rival and the first British cyclist in living memory to win an Olympic gold medal.

From her trackside seat in the back straight, with nearly as many cameras focused on her as on her husband, Sally had found herself at times unable to watch the race and was glad when it was over: 'The only thing I felt when he won was relief. If he had punctured, that would have been it.'

There by right – Boardman on the podium in Barcelona with silver medallist Jans Lehmann of Germany to his right and New Zealander, Gary Anderson taking the bronze, on his left.

Watching on television, there were only a few minutes for the family to celebrate alone before the by-now familiar faces of the reporters appeared at Olive's window, but this time the family didn't care. Olive put the kettle on and the journalists opened the champagne for the celebratory photos of the Boardmans in the morning papers. Their son was the Olympic champion, British cycling had its first gold medal from the Games for 72 years, Edward and Harriet had an Olympic champion for a dad, and the British press had their story. A 'superbike' that Chris Boardman had pedalled to Olympic gold and, according to some of them, a 'millionaire lifestyle'.

After passing Lehmann Chris circled the track twice, waving to the crowd before he stopped alongside Sally. 'It was a strange feeling. I wasn't overwhelmed by it – I couldn't really take it in at that time. I didn't think "that's it, I'm the Olympic champion". Not immediately, anyway.' Their trackside embrace featured in most of the newspapers. The reported 'You've done it, I love you' was the product of the fevered imagination of caption writers. 'We didn't say anything – there wasn't time. We only hugged each other for a moment,' says Sally.

Peter Keen, the man responsible for the training programme and who had forecast the Olympic gold for Chris, sat down in the track centre and tried to take it all in. 'I had prepared him for the victory – but I realized that I hadn't prepared myself for it. I just sat there, and thought, "it worked – it worked!". It was surreal.' Keen believes that Chris Boardman's belief in himself was crucial to his victory. 'What staggered me was how at ease he was with it. On the podium he looked like a man who felt he deserved to be there, not someone lucky to find himself there. There's an important difference.'

There was no time for Sally and Chris to celebrate the victory that night either, as he was riding in the team pursuit race less than 24 hours later. (The British team finished 8th – a result that somewhat took the shine off his personal triumph.) There were reports in some papers that they stood on the beach that night, discussing their future – but, sadly for those who like a romantic element to a story, this was not quite the case, as Sally wasn't there. 'It was Chris and Peter Keen. They were talking about the race and planning the next step,' she says.

The new Olympic champion had been unable to sleep. Retrieving his gold medal from underneath the pillow, he went with Peter to Barcelona's waterfront. The champion and his coach sat and talked about what they had achieved. 'It was the first time that I've ever relaxed to that extent; where I've shown emotion about winning.' Everything he had done up to that point had been part of a long term plan and although his many time trial, road race and track victories had given him satisfaction he had never really celebrated them. 'I always thought I would celebrate when I won something like the world championship or the Olympics – so I was prepared to feel good about this for a long time!'

Chris Boardman had taken the Olympic laurels, but he was not going to rest on them. Although he was enjoying the afterglow of victory, he was already thinking ahead to the next year's racing. He had said he was prepared to celebrate it, but Olympic champion was just a stage along the way. Throughout his career as he has achieved one ambition he has searched immediately for another. This time, though, before he could move on to the next step he would have to come to terms with his new life of Olympic champion, media personality and businessman.

On the night of his victory, Chris kept the gold medal under his pillow. There is now a small tooth mark where he reassured himself it was real.

CHAPTER FOUR

Record Return

RETURNING TRIUMPHANT FROM BARCELONA, Chris Boardman stepped from the plane at Manchester Airport a sporting celebrity who was – according to some of the more imaginative sections of the British press – already on the way to becoming a millionaire. From his welcome at Manchester Airport, Chris and his family were driven the 45 miles home to Wirral in a Lotus Carlton supplied by General Motors, the then parent company of Lotus, and on to a civic reception at Wirral Town Hall. The people of Hoylake had prepared a welcome for the new Olympic champion – the shops in the High Street were decorated in red, white and blue bunting, with photos of Chris in their windows. Banners across the road added to the carnival atmosphere, as did a street party outside Chris and Sally's home.

The media were out in force to greet the new Olympic champion, and images of the family reunion, with Chris holding his children, Edward and Harriet, and kissing Sally, were on television screens that evening and in the following day's newspapers. This was the beginning of a new life for Chris and his family – and it would take some getting used to. Three year-old Edward was not overly impressed by the men and women who had become a daily feature in his life. 'He told me he didn't like the "'porters", as he called them', says Sally. 'He didn't understand what was happening, just that his Dad had won a race.'

His Dad wasn't used to this kind of attention either. In the week after the final he had stayed in the Olympic Village, effectively cut off from reality and protected from the media. 'In a way I was expecting to come home and have a few people say, "Oh, I heard you did OK in that race". That's the way it had always been.' But an Olympic title ensured a transformation from a man whose fame was limited to the arcane world of cycle racing, to "Chris Boardman", the name that even people with no real interest in cycling now knew.

Local cyclists in Wirral had their chance to see Boardman for the first time since Barcelona when Ann and Neil Chapman organized an informal reception at their Eureka Café – the same venue that Chris had been going to since he was a baby with his parents. One of the crowd remembers Chris's return. 'He walked in with a big smile and just said "Coffee please, Ann".

ABOVE: *Sally, Harriet, Chris and Edward outside Manchester airport, the first of many photocalls for the newly-crowned Olympic champion.*

OPPOSITE: *Joy and pain – while Chris celebrates another success, this time breaking the 5,000 metre world record at the Leicester track in 1992, his son Edward is not so taken with the occasion.*

He wasn't affected by it at all.' But of course he was: 'It was a strange feeling. I was still the same person, but I felt like the old life had been taken away from me.' Chris also noticed that while some friends seemed awkward with him, unsure of how to approach him, others seemed more down to earth about it, and treated him as they always had done.

The mainstream cycling press were also aware of the changes taking place. Andrew Sutcliffe, editor of *Cycling Weekly*, wrote of his feelings in an article which captured perfectly the new life that Chris faced. As he waited to interview the new champion in Barcelona the day after the final, Sutcliffe was thinking how easy it had been to get hold of Chris in the days before Boardman became Olympic champion. But now it was all the high security, no access confines of the Olympic Village. Sutcliffe had to battle through a series of obstacles to talk to the man who, until a month previously, would have had difficulty getting even one daily newspaper interested in him! Now they all wanted to know Boardman, and not only the newspapers were wooing him. When Sutcliffe first tried to contact him Boardman was at lunch with David Mellor, the then Government minister whose National Heritage portfolio covered sport.

Sutcliffe eventually managed to get his interview, although he did have some fears. 'Fame is a funny thing', he wrote 'I start to worry that he's going to appear with half a dozen minders. What if he wants cash for having his picture taken? Have I got enough money?'

There was no need for these concerns. Chris arrived 'minder'-less (apart from Peter Keen) and, despite a slightly distant, dazed appearance, he was his usual self as he spoke about winning the Olympic title and his future plans. The journalist wondered how Chris was going to capitalize on his success. The banner headline in one daily, 'You'll earn a million', prompted Sutcliffe to write 'How? Tell me how. He must support his wife and children. Perhaps he can sign off the dole? There are lots of problems. The first sharks have been sighted. He is entering a new world, an uncharted world, and he needs a map.'

Boardman and Keen had attempted to chart such a map to help them plan the racer's career in the immediate future, and how it could be fitted in to make the most of the massive publicity that he had received; he had to earn a living. Before Barcelona he wasn't available for work due to his racing commitments, so couldn't even claim benefit. At Barcelona, the Olympic champion and his coach made the decision that while it was important to develop any business opportunity, his racing career should not suffer as a result.

As far as racing was concerned the next step was also planned in Barcelona. 'We decided while we were there to try to retake the 5,000 metre amateur world record,' says Chris. He had set this record at Leicester in 1991 clocking 5 minutes, 47.70 seconds during his preparation for Stuttgart and the world championship pursuit title. Two months later it was taken from him by the American, Kent Bostick, who had covered the distance in 5 minutes, 46 seconds.

Chris decided to return to Leicester once more to attack the record during the British track championship week at the end of August 1992, but was aware that it would not be easy. Bostick had improved on Boardman's time at altitude. Attacking altitude records at sea level was seen by many as pointless because of the benefits gained at high altitude, where the rider's ability to use oxygen is enhanced, giving him an advantage.

Nevertheless, Leicester was chosen as Chris would be there to defend his British pursuit title –

but there was an additional reason. 'We wanted to do something for the crowd at Leicester and the world record attempt seemed a good idea.' These plans were made before he returned home to England.

Within 24 hours of becoming Olympic champion offers began arriving at the Boardman's home. When Sally returned from Barcelona she began dealing with them. There were often 30 letters and as many phone calls a day to answer, as well as looking after two small children. Both she and Chris knew that they needed a manager to handle his career and after considering some of the offers Chris decided to take the safe option of choosing a friend of the family to advise him.

Harry Middleton is a businessman and racing cyclist who has known Keith and Carol Boardman since the early 1960s. He had faxed Chris after the Olympic final to congratulate him and also to let him know that, if he wanted, he could introduce him to some of his business contacts. At this point Harry had no intention of becoming Chris Boardman's manager. 'I just wanted to see if I could do something for him by putting him in touch with people who could help him.'

At the end of August Harry had a phone call from Chris and they arranged to meet to discuss what he had to offer. When he sent the fax to Chris, Harry Middleton was planning his semi-retirement from business. Two months later he was

The press called the shots in the latter part of 1992 when Chris found his diary full of personal appearances, one which involved setting a 5,000 metre record on an exercise bike in one of London's exclusive health clubs.

Chris Boardman's manager. 'I told Chris I'd never done anything quite like this before,' says Harry, 'but I said that if he felt I could help him I would.'

As far as Chris was concerned Harry was the safe option. 'I preferred to have someone that I knew and trusted. I'd had other offers, but thought it would be best with Harry.'

Many people in the cycling world believed that Chris should have turned professional immediately after Barcelona. There were claims in some newspapers that 'contracts worth £750,000 were waiting for him' but this was not quite the case. 'In the cycling world, Barcelona meant very little to potential sponsors,' says Chris. Team managers in Europe watch carefully for signs of potential greatness in young amateur riders. An Olympic pursuit title, while useful in that it sends out a clear signal of a rider's potential, does not mean a guaranteed entry to one of the major teams. Chris did have one offer from a major British sponsor which he turned down because of his own drive and ambition. 'It appealed to me because I could stay with the family, but riding as a professional here would be a cop out. It doesn't mean anything to say you are the best pro in Britain.' By this Chris was referring to the state of the home professional scene, which had fewer than 30 registered riders, only one major team and placed a general public perception that cycling traditionally somewhere between morris dancing and tiddlywinks. The recession would not help either as any potential sponsors of the British professional cycling scene were not prepared to invest money in teams.

However, life as a professional in a continental European team holds equally little appeal for Boardman. Because the team managers would not be overly impressed by the Olympic title, Chris's bargaining power would only be strong enough to secure him a place just above that of a *domestique*,

(literally 'servant') – the workhorses of the team. The duties of the *domestiques* are to ensure that the team leader has as easy a ride as possible, protecting him in the *peloton* (the bunch of riders), fetching him water bottles from the team car when needed and generally doing everything they can to look after the team's star man until he gets on with the business of winning the race. This kind of riding did not appeal to Chris at all.

The lack of bargaining power in team duties was a factor in Chris's decision not to turn professional immediately after Barcelona. It certainly seemed perverse that the Olympic Games which made Boardman's name well known outside cycling did not mean as much to the continental

Chris prepares for the 5,000 metre record at Leicester in August 1992 while the LotusSport inventor Mike Burrows looks on. This was to be Chris's final appearance on the black superbike.

managers. Regarded as the 'blue riband' by fans, riders, and most importantly, by team managers, the holder of the world hour record can name his price in negotiations and while this was important, the 'hour' meant more than that to Chris. 'It's the ultimate record. Its history, and the names of the riders who have held it, say it all'.

In the autumn of 1992 as Chris was formulating ideas about how, when and where he would make his record attempt, it became clear that there were problems in the relationship with Lotus. Prior to the Barcelona Olympics, Chris had dealt mainly with the engineers of the Norwich company as they fine-tuned the prototypes. But now top-level management was involved, the business negotiations got more complicated, and the once good relationship began to sour. The chief sticking point was Chris's business agreement with Preston-based Ribble Cycles, signed in January 1992, to ride their bikes for his amateur club, the Stoke-based GS Strada. Lotus management were not prepared to talk to Chris until after 1 January 1993 when his contract with Ribble ran out.

For the Barcelona Olympics this sticking point had been smoothed over by the British Cycling Federation acting as mediator and officially 'adopting' a Lotus bike for the Olympics and then 'selecting' a rider to wear the BCF's red, white and blue colours. This effectively had been the only way Chris was able to use the Lotus bike in competition – and now Lotus were using the Ribble contract as a reason for not talking to Chris.

In between such delicate negotiations and handling his new life of personal appearances – travelling the length and breadth of the country opening supermarkets, supporting charity events and recording television programmes – Chris tried to keep on top of his training schedule. For a rider who had been so single-minded, this aspect

team managers, whereas the world hour record, which would impress them, would not mean much, if anything at all, to the non-cyclists who applauded his Barcelona victory.

In 1991 during the preparation for the world championship Chris had considered an attempt on the hour record. He didn't go for it then, but 12 months later he and Peter Keen began to view this not only as the next step in his career but as the means of attracting the attention of the team

Riding on form from the Olympics and urged on by a large and enthusiastic crowd, Chris smashes the 5,000 metre world record at the Leicester track. It was to be his last serious track race of the 1992 season.

of his new life was a problem. 'I couldn't train properly. It was just damage control really.' Any training that he did manage was fitted in during the drive to and from his engagements. 'We would stop the car and I would get changed and go off and do two hours' riding,' says Chris. 'It was a lot of messing around, so it wasn't the best preparation.' This type of training would probably be enough for an amateur rider hoping to do well in a 10-mile club race, but Chris Boardman's next target was the 5,000 metre world record.

When he had first broken it 12 months earlier Chris had travelled to Leicester in anonymity. Now, on 20 August 1992 the demands of his new life saw him stopping off in the city to open a new superstore before going on to the velodrome. Two thousand people turned out to see Chris's attempt to regain the world record – many more than

would normally be expected at the Saffron Lane stadium.

One week earlier he had raced at Leicester to win the British amateur pursuit title on his conventional track bike, but for the record attempt he would be reunited with the Lotus for the first time since the Olympics – again wearing the BCF 'colours of convenience' to get round the contractual complications between Ribble and Lotus (rather than the colours of his team, GS Strada). He didn't know it then, but this would be the last time he would use the Lotus in competition. The Lotus bike never actually belonged to Chris: immediately after the Olympic pursuit final it had been whisked away by engineers from the company. The next time Chris saw it was just before his record attempt began. Although the knowledgeable cycling fans understood that it was Chris, not the bike, that had won the gold medal at Barcelona, there was still a lot of interest in the machine.

Chris was going for a record that was 1,000 metres further than his specialist distance and had prepared what Doug Dailey describes as an 'audacious' schedule to beat it. But conditions were far from ideal: there was a strong cold wind, and the rain clouds hung ominously overhead. It was going to be difficult, he knew. 'I had been watching a four-man team pursuit earlier, and they were really struggling. It put it into perspective when I realized I would have to go faster than that by myself'.

The threat of rain presented further problems. The wooden track cannot be used in wet conditions, so the attempt would have to be postponed. According to his schedule, Chris needed only 5 minutes and 42 seconds of dry weather to beat the record. At 1:45pm, with the sky darkening and the wind growing stronger, the solitary figure on the track began his record attempt.

The expectant crowd cheered on the Olympic champion in action and within one lap he was half a second up on his schedule – a lead that would grow steadily. At the one kilometre mark he was two seconds ahead, the stopwatch recording

1 minute, 10 seconds. The crowd were right behind him now, those on the front row leaning over and hammering their fists on the wooden boards of the perimeter fence to spur him on.

With 3,000 metres covered, Chris was five seconds up on his schedule – a lead he would extend by four more seconds over the final two kilometres. He crossed the finish line to an enormous roar from the crowd. He had beaten the amateur world 5,000 metre record by the huge margin of nine seconds, with a time of 5 minutes 38.083 seconds, which amazingly also bettered the professional figures set by Germany's Gregor Braun.

He had wanted to do something for the support back home, and everyone agreed that he had done just that. 'It was a way of saying thanks to everyone here who has helped me out this year,'

Talking to the crowd after breaking the 5,000 metre record. At the time, despite his Olympic gold, Chris was still very ambivalent about a professional career.

Riding a Ribble machine, the bike he was contracted to ride for his amateur club, Chris salutes the crowd after breaking the 5,000 metre record.

said Chris immediately afterwards. Ironically, the one person who was truly instrumental in his succes was not there. Peter Keen had been held up in a 15-mile traffic jam on the M1, where he fumed silently, wondering how his rider was doing.

In an interview shortly afterwards Boardman, surrounded by well-wishers and autograph hunters, responded to questions about the attempt and about his future plans – the most immediate of which involved escaping to the Lake District with family and friends for a short holiday. 'We needed a break from it all', says Chris of that period. 'It was so busy that it took some getting used to, but even on holiday we had to take a portable phone.' Such were the trappings of the new life for the Boardmans. Six weeks earlier they could have gone away for as long as they wished and the world at large wouldn't have been bothered. Now handfuls of letters arrived every day and the phone never stopped ringing with all kinds of offers, ranging from the bizarre (racing against a horse as part of a corporate day out) to the worthy (acting as a spokesperson on health and fitness for Mersey Regional Health), to the mundane (calling out the numbers at a bingo session and opening supermarkets).

The Lake District holiday would give Chris and Sally a chance to sit back and relax, but it would also allow them to go through a growing pile of potential deals, including several offers of management from prospective business partners. Typically, it rained throughout their summer holiday week. Chris didn't do any cycling but tried to keep up on his fitness by swimming and joining a gym. At the swimming pool with Sally he became aware of the celebrity tag he had recently acquired. A group of people recognized him and a crowd gathered to watch the Olympic pursuit champion swimming. 'It was really funny,' says Sally. 'One of them said "Ooh, isn't he white". They must have thought he could have done some sunbathing while he was in Barcelona.'

The people who used the gym were not as quick as those in the pool in spotting Chris. Had they done so it might have saved their egos after Chris had pushed the exercise bike beyond its limit. 'It was set up to allow you to go for a record distance over five minutes,' says the fastest man in the world at this particular exercise. 'You are supposed to add your name to the list on the wall if you beat the best distance… but I didn't bother to do that.' Lycra-bound keep-fit aficionados watched their performances shattered by a man who, if compared to their own iron-pumped and suntanned torsos, looked ordinary in the extreme. It was only at the end of the week when they actually recognized who Chris was that their bruised egos were restored.

This was one of the last times in 1992 that Boardman's legs were pedalled at any intensity. He rode only two more races that year: an invitation time trial in which he punctured after 20 miles and didn't finish, and a hill climb race, where he finished second.

The break in the Lake District marked the end of Sally's 'management' of her husband's career as Harry Middleton took over at the end of August. From September through to Christmas, Chris was involved in some form of appearance or interview every other day. There were some in the cycling world who were surprised at some of the appearances that Boardman made during this period; but there was a reason. Following the Barcelona

Olympics, Raleigh Cycles commissioned a survey to find out what people remembered of the Olympics, and in particular the pursuit race. The results suggested that four people out of five remembered the Lotus bike, while only one in five remembered Chris Boardman. Appearing on TV programmes such *The Big Breakfast*, *Noel's House Party* and *A Question of Sport* was part of a plan to make Chris Boardman's face as well known as his name.

One of Harry Middleton's business associates is Alan Dunn, a former racing cyclist who Harry has known since the late 1950s. Dunn's racing was curtailed when he became road manager of the Rolling Stones, with whom he has worked since 1965. With advice from Dunn, Chris's image was 'groomed' with an eye on the prestigious BBC Sports Personality Award to be presented in December.

Cycling Weekly's Luke Evans accompanied Chris and Harry during a day of appointments in London, the busy schedule an example of Boardman's post-Olympic life. Monday 23 November saw Chris making a personal appearance at a health club to launch a computerized exercise bike. He was to set a time for 4,000 metres on the machine. If anyone could beat – or get near the time – they would receive free membership to the club. Suffering from a chest infection, with the effort showing on his face he finished the distance in 5 minutes, 33 seconds. 'When you're ill you can't just say "forget it" said Chris of his new commitments.

Fifteen minutes after finishing the exercise bike 'record attempt' he 'performed' once more, this time for the newspaper photographers who insist on an outside 'location shot'. The bike was positioned on a traffic island during the morning rush hour with Chris astride it, patiently waiting while the photographers got their shots.

Later that morning Chris and Harry had a meeting with a PR adviser who had been brought in to help raise the rider's profile in the last month before the BBC Sports Personality Award. It was not good news. She told them that this year they were probably too late as the other contenders' campaigns had built up too much of a lead. They decided to continue with the TV appearances already lined up, including *Blue Peter* later that day. At 2:15 a taxi arrived at the hotel to take Chris and Harry to the BBC studios. At 5:00pm the famous signature tune alerted the nation's watching kids that *Blue Peter* has started. The producer wanted Chris to ride a bike on stage, something Chris

wasn't keen to do because of his contract with Ribble. A compromise was reached and the offending trade name was taped over; Chris did his bit and was even awarded the coveted galleon badge!

Fifteen minutes later another taxi whisked the Boardman party to the Café Royal for the press launch of a fundraising campaign for the 1994 Commonwealth Games. After publicity photos of the athletes have been taken and speeches made, Chris and Harry are driven back to Heathrow for the shuttle back to Manchester.

Such appearances on TV and at press launches didn't hold any fears for Chris. 'An Olympic title gives you an incredible amount of self-confidence. It means that you meet a lot of people on equal terms, but also it justifies thing that I'd said or done in the past,' says Chris. 'Before Barcelona people may have dismissed my ideas, but since then people are more willing to listen to what I have to say.'

However, there was one TV appearance where his self-confidence evaporated in an instant. Appearing on *A Question of Sport* in October 1992, Chris fluffed a question on his own discipline of pursuit racing – the

From embrocation to foundation – the trappings of a television personality were a world apart for someone more used to changing in the back of a car and rubbing pungent embrocation into his legs!

supposedly easy round! 'It was just one of those things that can happen,' he says. 'It was a bit embarrassing, but nothing to lose sleep over.'

In an age when many celebrities are famous simply for being famous, with no apparent reason

*All smiles for the camera on the BBC's **Blue Peter**, where Chris, with co-presenter Diane-Louise Jordan, promoted a safety campaign for young cyclists in November 1992.*

for their constant television appearances, it must have been an attractive proposition for a man who had spent many years struggling to support his wife and children to put his cycling career on hold for a year or two while he capitalized on the publicity that came with Olympic gold. 'I could see that a living could be made doing that,' admitted Chris, 'but it would involve sacrifices in my racing, and there is no knowing how long a celebrity career can last.'

Boardman quickly decided against the celebrity option and a life of TV and bank holiday entertainment shows, instead he sat down with Peter Keen to discuss the only real option, that of furthering his racing career using the Olympic title as a stepping stone. There was only one way that

this could be achieved, given that he did not want to take on a support role in a continental European team, or turn professional in Britain.

The world hour record would be the means of grabbing the attention of the world's top team managers. If Chris could take it he would be in a position to negotiate a good contract in a strong team. The hour record, held since 1984 by the Italian Francesco Moser, would be Chris's target for 1993.

CHAPTER FIVE

Power of the Hour

THE WORLD OF CYCLING has been captivated by the hour record for over 100 years. It is the sport's 'Blue Riband', the maker or breaker of reputations. On 11 May 1893, Henri Desgrange, the Frenchman who later founded the Tour de France, pedalled his heavy steel bicycle around the Buffalo Stadium in Paris. At the end of his hour Desgrange had covered 35.325 kilometres. Since Desgrange, only 19 men had put their reputation on the line and captured the record for themselves. The last of these had been Francesco Moser, who in January 1984 was the first rider to shatter the magic distance of 50 kilometres.

Almost a century after Desgrange's pioneering effort, Chris Boardman entered the final phase of his attempt to smash Moser's seemingly unchallengeable distance. Chris did not know it then, but it would not be Francesco Moser's record that he would take later that year.

Two years earlier Boardman and his coach Peter Keen had prepared an outline for an attempt on 'the hour' as part of the rider's preparation for the ill-fated world championship in Stuttgart. They had considered going for Moser's record at Leicester during the British Championship week, but postponed it in favour of the successful 5,000 metres attempt. Nobody would have blamed Chris if he had not taken things any further than that. Boardman was good, there was no doubting that, but was he in the same league as riders such as Coppi, Merckx or Moser, three of the most famous holders of the record in the last 50 years?

The history of the hour record after Desgrange jumps to World War Two and Fausto Coppi – known to his fans as the *campionissimo*, 'the champion of champions'. In 1942, shortly before he was conscripted by the Italian army, Coppi covered 45.848 kilometres on Milan's Vigorelli track. The great Italian, whose career was temporarily halted when he became a POW of the British Army in North Africa, kept his record for 14 years. In 1956 Jacques Anquetil, a young French rider who later achieved the same legendary status as Coppi, set a new figure of 46.159 kilometres, once again in Milan. The Vigorelli stadium was the venue for every successful record attempt from 1935 to 1958, and in 1956 the Italian, Ercole Baldini, raced around its banked concrete surface to become the first amateur to hold the hour record.

ABOVE: *Eddy Merckx, unquestionably the best rider of his day, added his name to the hour record holders in 1972.*

OPPOSITE: *The man to beat – Francesco Moser may have been at the end of his career but that was not evident in Mexico in 1984 when the big Italian broke the 51km barrier for the hour record.*

71

In 1957 the record was reclaimed by the professionals when a 21 year-old Frenchman, Roger Riviere, beat Baldini's figures to set a new distance of 46.923 kilometres. Less than 12 months later he improved it to 47.346 kilometres. In 1961 it seemed that Riviere had the world at his feet. He had started that year's Tour de France as favourite to win, when he misjudged a corner on a dangerous Pyrennean descent and plunged 90 feet into a rock-strewn ravine. He survived the fall, but his back was broken and he never raced again.

Jacques Anquetil returned to claim the record in 1966, only to have it disallowed by UCI officials when he refused an obligatory drug test, so it was not until 1967 that Riviere's figures were bettered, this time by the Belgian rider Ferdi Bracke. One year later Bracke flew to Mexico City with the intention of beating his own record at the brand new Olympic velodrome. He succeeded, and the use of a track at altitude set a precedent for future hour-record aspirants, including the Danish rider Ole Ritter, who followed Bracke to Mexico at the end of 1968 and relieved him of his newly-won record.

Ritter could claim to be the fastest man in the world for the next four years, although everybody who had an interest in cycling believed that he was merely looking after the record until Eddy Merckx decided that the time was right for him to go for the 'blue riband'. In October 1972, once again in Mexico, Merckx covered 49.431 kilometres in one hour. This performance was hailed as the record to beat all records – and for 12 years remained so.

Roger Riviere's tragically short career included two updates of the hour record. Had he not been paralyzed by a racing crash he would have almost certainly added a third.

In January 1984 the 'unchallengeable record' was destroyed by a man thought to be nearing the end of a victory-laden racing career. Francesco Moser had been hailed as Italy's new *campionissimo*, although in cycle racing's hall of fame he would perhaps be found in a side lobby. But his exploits in January 1984 will ensure that he will be forever known as the man who not only beat Merckx's record, but who brought the 'hour', and with it all forms of cycle racing, into the age of technology.

Riding a bicycle that astounded the cycling world with its low-profile design and oversized rear disc wheel, and trained 'scientifically' by his personal adviser, Dr Conconi, Moser broke the 50 kilometre barrier. The news was still being discussed by fans who argued that this 50.808 kilometres must surely be the limit when, four days later, Moser returned to Mexico's Olympic velodrome and really gave them something to talk about. He went even further, and journalists ran out of superlatives as they tried to convey the magnitude of his achievement. A matter of a few days previously they were writing that 50.808 kilometres would never be beaten, and now Francesco had done just that, racing to a new record of 51.151 kilometres .

Cycling fans around the world marvelled at the new record and at the man who had set it: Eddie Soens enthused about it to a 15 year-old Boardman. Although the hour record did not at that time feature in Boardman's plans, Peter Keen, then a 19-year old undergraduate, did entertain such thoughts. 'I was racing then and I used to dream about one day taking the record, but that's all it was – a dream,' he says. 'But I do remember thinking quite seriously that I would like to be involved in preparing a rider for the record.' And this is where Peter found himself at the start of 1993.

Chris had made the hour his target for that year, after his manager, Harry Middleton, convinced Chris of the importance and standing of the record. 'Chris wanted to make the world championship his

Italian Ercole Baldini, perhaps not best dressed for the occasion, demonstrates his power output in 1956 on a static bike while a white-coated technician monitors the controls.

aim for the year,' says Harry. 'I told him that if people had to name the last five world pursuit champions, they would have difficulty, but they would remember the holders of the hour record. It means so much more'.

Convinced by Middleton that the 'hour' must take precedence in his programme, Chris was then persuaded by Peter Keen that he could actually do it. Early in the new year, Boardman travelled to Brighton to meet Keen at the college where he now taught. 'We sat in a lecture room for three hours and Peter filled a board with figures that explained why it was feasible that I could do it,' said Chris, who at this point was still not entirely won over. This was chiefly because Keen's calculations for success were based on the power (in terms of wattage produced by man and machine) that he would have to turn out for the 60 minutes on the Kingcycle rig Keen had set up for scientific training. In recent trials on the rig Chris had not performed as well as he would have liked. 'I hadn't been able to hold 400 watts for 10 minutes, and Peter was telling me that I would have to hold 430 for an hour to beat the record!'.

But Peter Keen possesses the qualities and skills essential to anybody involved in the training of athletes. He has the ability to motivate a rider, persuading them with argument and physiological reasoning that they can achieve an aim. He went through every aspect of Moser's 1984 performance, analyzing the Italian's physique and abilities, evaluating the bike and equipment that he used, comparing them with Chris's, and generally psyching up his rider. After the mathematical reasoning this was the spur that Chris needed. 'By the time Peter had finished I was convinced that we could do it,' he says. 'The real planning for the hour record began that day.'

As the decision was made to begin this preparation, storm clouds were gathering over the Boardman-Lotus relationship. Despite the fact that Chris's agreement with Ribble Cycles had ended on 1 January 1993, the Norwich-based company were still circumspect in their dealings with him.

The attempts by Harry Middleton to secure a contract with Lotus had come to noth-

One of the great time triallists of all time, Jacques Anquetil (pictured here in 1964) attacked the hour record and bettered Coppi's distance in 1956. But when the Frenchman went for the record two years later he refused to attend a dope test and the figures were disallowed.

ing. The deal they offered Chris was, according to his manager, nothing more than potential earnings from the marketing of a superbike replica and associated merchandise which at that point were not in production. The Christmas market had been missed, and in an age of fleeting interests there was no guarantee that a replica of the winning bike would sell once the public's memories of Chris's Olympic victory began to fade. When Chris rejected this proposal Lotus released a statement describing him as unreasonable for turning down a lucrative offer. This was not how Boardman saw it.

Patrick Peal, Head of Communications at Lotus, points out that at that time the company was going through a difficult period, a factor that Chris was aware of. 'If they had said "we can offer you this now, stick with us and we can review it next year" I would have gone for that,' he says. 'It was their total lack of respect for what I had achieved that I found hard to take.'

Peal insists that it was a good offer and believes that there was a 'mis-match of aspirations' in the negotiations, but if this was the case there was also a mis-match of benefits received. From the middle of July 1992 Lotus received

worldwide publicity, the cost of which can only be guessed at – something which Lotus acknowledge: 'We couldn't put a price on publicity like that,' says Peal. 'Just think of a number and add lots of millions to it.'

The final straw came at a meeting with the company directors to discuss a contract and the use of a LotusSport for the hour record attempt. 'At the end of the meeting, when they had been hostile all the way through, one of them asked me if I really believed I could get the hour record without the bike!' says Chris. By this time he was already losing patience with some of the extravagant claims emanating from Lotus about the effect of their bike on his performance in Barcelona.

It seemed that some of the Lotus management had begun to believe their own publicity and, convinced that Boardman's success was due to the superbike (despite conflicting evidence when other British riders used the machine) Lotus gave Chris the impression that they felt that he should

By June 1993 Chris was approaching his best ever form. Defending his 25-mile national title was all part of the build up for the hour record and winning the 25-mile title in record time confirmed that everything was on target.

be grateful to be involved and that the loan of the bike was a good enough deal in itself.

More recently, however, Lotus have re-appraised their initial judgement on the effect of their bike on Boardman's performance. Peal says: 'We know what the value of the bike was, in terms of seconds per kilometre, and Chris made full use of that. He probably would have won the gold medal on a kid's tricycle, he was so committed.'

Although Chris felt that he was capable of getting the hour record without the LotusSport he still wanted to use the bike in trials to see how it compared to other machines. In the initial euphoria after Barcelona he had been swept along, like everybody else, by the speculation over just how aerodynamic the Lotus was. He had since had time to

Riding a fixed gear to simulate his track machine, Chris smashed his own 25-mile record in May 1993. He improved 1 minute, 22 seconds on his old record of the year before, setting new figures of 45 minutes, 57 seconds.

reflect and could now make a realistic assessment. 'I would guess it was worth two or three seconds over the 4,000 metres. It was certainly the most aerodynamic bike at the time, but I doubt some of the figures that were put around then,' he says.

In addition to the wrangling over a sponsorship deal, Lotus were reluctant to allow Chris and Peter Keen to borrow the bike for track trials scheduled for May in Bordeaux, claiming that they were not given sufficient notice to prepare the machine. Halfords had bought one of the five Lotus prototypes for display purposes and they were approached by Harry Middleton. 'They were more than willing to help us, so we thought we

would have the bike for the trials,' said Harry. 'Two days later they phoned back and said it could be awkward for them to loan it to Chris.' Likewise, the Science Museum were unwilling to part with their loaned prototype.

Harry, Chris and Peter drew their own conclusions and arranged to use other bikes for the tests. An American Zipp, French Corima and two English Cougar track machines, one low profile, the other conventional, were transported to Bordeaux in May for the first trials. 'It was a pity we didn't have a Lotus,' says Chris. 'We would have been willing to use it regardless of all the problems if it had proved to be the best.'

All four bikes were evaluated in a series of carefully monitored tests devised by Peter Keen. The data was analyzed and the Corima proved the most efficient of the bikes available. Corima specialize in carbon fibre construction and were asked to supply a bike based on the one used in the trials.

The new Corima, a gleaming yellow carbon fibre machine, was taken to Bordeaux on 23 June, where Chris used it during a week's training. From the world class indoor timber velodrome at Bordeaux, the bike was flown back to Britain and at Kirkby stadium outside Liverpool Chris rode a 20-minute trial on the outdoor, windswept tarmac cycle track. The only people to witness his 51.7 kilometres-per-hour performance were a group of schoolchildren practising for their sports day, but afterwards Chris knew that he and the Corima were ready to perform in front of a much larger audience.

But by now Boardman also knew that he was not the only man with his sights set on Francesco Moser's title. Two weeks earlier Graeme Obree had announced that he would be going for the record.

Graeme Obree and Chris Boardman had raced against each other in time trials since 1990, but whether by design or accident they did not meet regularly. The interest caused by these clashes had a lot to do with the uncertainty of the result, as Obree constantly pushed Chris, always threatening to beat him. However, there was another reason for the interest, and that was curiosity about Obree himself.

The Scotsman appears to be a maverick, with a laid-back attitude to his racing and training, and then there are those that feel that the impression that the Scot gives is not quite accurate, that despite his apparent relaxed complacency towards his racing, Obree is every bit as motivated and dedicated as any elite athlete.

But the factor that sets him apart from his rivals is his bike and the unorthodox riding position that he has developed. While conventional drop handlebars have been superseded in time trials by the triathlon type, Obree had designed his position to be even more aerodynamic. He presents an unusual sight as he leans forward on his flat handlebars, arms tucked completely under his chest and head lolling over the front wheel of his strange-looking machine.

When photographs first appeared of this man who was regularly winning Scottish time trials, people reacted in the way they often do when confronted with something out of the ordinary - they laughed. When Obree travelled south and began winning time trials in England, the laughter was replaced with curiosity and later, respect.

For some enthusiasts these clashes were a battle between what they saw as the quasi-professional Boardman, with his high-tech, dedicated approach to the sport, and the 'easy come, easy go' Scottish amateur who raced simply for his love of time trialling. In 1990 the pair met at Newtownards in Northern Ireland for the prestigious 25-mile race held there each May. Obree beat Boardman for the first time, and the result prompted one cyclist to write to *Cycling Weekly*, telling the magazine that Boardman's defeat had not just made his day, but his week!

In 1989 Obree had broken the British hour record, held since 1973 by the professional rider Dave Lloyd. A year later he improved his own figures to 46.390 kilometres, and was candid

The Tour of Lancashire gave Chris particular satisfaction as, for the second time in his career, he fended off UK-based pros. But road racing played a small part in his preparation for the hour record and world championships in 1993.

developing his ideas in the unique riding position that he had pioneered, designing and building his own bicycle frames.

Obree's motivation to return to top level racing was provided when Chris Boardman won the Olympic gold medal. Reasoning that before his 'retirement' he was only a little way behind Chris, Obree began his preparation for the 1993 season. He was now a member of a sponsored team based in London, and much of his racing would be in England. As the Boardman camp prepared for a season based on taking the world hour record, Obree drew up his own schedule for the year.

Despite Chris's fears that his winter as a 'celebrity' had undermined his preparation, his race results were encouraging. He had returned to the club that he had joined as a 13 year-old, the North Wirral Velo, bringing with him a sponsorship deal with Kodak and Reebok. The biggest success of the early part of the season was his victory in the Tour of Lancashire, a repeat performance of his classic 1991 win. Just as the year before, all his races were aimed at a specific target, his whole season revolving around the Hour record. As well as road races like the Lancashire Tour, time trials were used to put a fine edge to his speed. Riding a bike with one fixed gear, similar to the one he would use in the hour attempt, Chris returned to his racing roots and the local 10 mile time trials. 'It was an ideal way for me to have a

about his reasons, telling a journalist afterwards: 'Chris Boardman was the main factor in my doing it again. He said he was going to beat it, and he is my main man.'

Obree's 'main man' has a respect for the Scot, but he is not as caught up in a rivalry as journalists like to portray. As far as Boardman is concerned, Graeme Obree is just one of many competitors that he races against. If there was a rivalry between the two men it appeared to have dissolved in June 1991 when Obree announced that he was quitting the British Olympic squad and would continue racing at a less demanding level.

Throughout the rest of 1991 and most of the 1992 season Obree did just that – but as he concentrated on his new bike shop business he was also

*Chris and Brian Smith battle it out on Jeffrey Hill in the 1993
Tour of Lancashire. Smith, from Scotland, was one of the top
UK pros that year, and in 1994 he followed Boardman to the
continent, signing for the US-backed Motorola team.*

"level three" training session', says Boardman. 'It's psychologically easier to do it in race conditions and makes a change from the usual training.' Many of the riders there would remember Chris as the skinny 13 year-old who wanted to race just to see what it was like. Now he was using these races as preparation for the ultimate test.

Obree was also gearing up for his attempt on the hour. At the end of May he improved his British hour record. Two weeks later on 6 June he and Chris lined up for the National 25 Mile Championship, held at Redruth in Cornwall. It was always going to be a close race between the two. Seven days earlier Chris had set a new British record of 45 minutes, 57 seconds, a clear sign of his fitness and intent. The final result – Boardman winning in 48 minutes, 45 seconds, 10 seconds clear of Obree – may have turned out differently. The Scot had to stop with mechanical problems before half distance, when he was reportedly 24 seconds faster than Boardman, and Chris is realistic about the outcome if this hadn't happened.

After the race the talk turned to the goal that both men were chasing. Obree told journalists that he was looking for a good track and that he hoped to get the record before Chris made his attempt.

Chris and his team of advisers had already decided which velodrome they would use. After considering the high altitude track at Colorado Springs, USA, as a possibility it was suggested by Peter Woodworth, a member of Chris's support team, that the indoor velodrome in Bordeaux would be ideal. It didn't have the main advantage of Colorado as it was at sea level, but would be much easier to organize and to travel to. There was another major advantage in using Bordeaux's Le Lac velodrome. The 18th stage of the Tour de France would be finishing just outside the stadium and the world's media would have their attention firmly fixed on Bordeaux on Friday 23 July, the date that Boardman and his team had targetted. Also, critically, the world's top cycling teams and their managers would be there. This would be the best possible way for Chris to show his potential employers what he was capable of, and what he would be worth as a professional rider.

Peter Woodworth had taken on the co-ordination of the hour record attempt to allow Harry Middleton to concentrate on running both his own business and the North Wirral Velo-Kodak team – a full time job in itself due to their race programme. In a training session at Bordeaux at the end of June, riding the bright yellow Corima, Boardman broke Francesco Moser's 10 kilometre world record. There were no UCI officials present, so it was unofficial, but the time of 11 minutes, 28 seconds (22 seconds better than Moser's) signalled that Chris was on target. There were just over four weeks to go.

At the same time Graeme Obree was stepping up his preparation. The week before Chris beat the 10 kilometre record, the Scot set a new British record for 10 miles, riding the distance in 18 minutes, 27 seconds. The following day he won the British 50-mile Championship, once again setting a new British record.

Chris's last race before his third and final journey to Bordeaux was the British team time trial championship, the 100 kilometre race where four members of the same team relay each other. The North Wirral Velo-Kodak team of Chris, Paul Jennings, Simon Lillistone and Peter Longbottom won the championship in a time of 2 hours and 7 seconds, more than nine minutes clear of the second placed team. The Olympic champion's own form was evident. Speaking afterwards, he said that he was 'comfortable' during the race, despite a 20-mile section covered at 39 miles per hour.

This race, and every other that he had won in the year, faded into insignificance as Chris flew out to Bordeaux with Peter Woodworth. There would be two weeks of preparation to put the final edge on his fitness. The back-up team of Peter Keen and Paul Jennings would drive the 800 miles with all the necessary equipment and spare bikes, while David O'Brien, Chris's longtime cycling friend, would arrive later to act as mechanic.

There had been a problem in finding a suitable vehicle for the transportation until Alan Dunn came to the rescue. Despite a full-time occupation managing the Rolling Stones on tour, Alan had always kept up his interest in cycling, and when he heard that the team were looking for a vehicle he was glad to help out. 'I spoke to Mick [Jagger] to see if they could use one of the company vans. He agreed, so they took it'.

As Keen and Jennings drove through Customs at Dover the van was singled out for a check by officials. 'They asked if it was our van so we told them no, it wasn't,' says Keen. 'Then we realized we didn't have any documents with us'. They tried explaining that they were going to Bordeaux to help Chris Boardman in a record attempt, but the officers were not impressed. They asked Jennings who the van belonged to. 'You're probably not going to believe this, but it's Mick Jagger's....' he told the officer, whose face by this time bore a 'Yes, I'm sure it is sir' expression. They were eventually

Showing fatigue from two attempts in 24 hours, a jubilant Obree is held aloft by a team helper, Andy Sharpe, after breaking the hour record on 17 July 1993.

allowed through after the arrival of another officer who had read about the attempt. 'Isn't it that guy in the pointy hat who won the Olympics?' was how he remembered Chris. Such is fame.

The pressure was beginning to build up within the group as 23 July drew closer, and some of this pressure was caused by the fact that everyone involved at Bordeaux knew that at some stage Graeme Obree was going to make his attempt on Moser's record. Obree had planned to go on the same track as Chris after he read that he had been pleased with his trials there, but a mix-up in the Scot's negotiations with the owners of the track meant that Obree had to travel to the Hamar stadium located in Norway instead.

On 16 July Chris had just finished a training session when he heard the news that Obree had failed in his attempt to take Moser's record. 'I was glad he hadn't done it, because it meant that I would be going for Moser's record, which was the original intention.' Obree's immediate announcement that he would try again the next day also did not worry Chris. Like most who were following the events, he thought it unlikely that Obree could recover in time.

But that's exactly what he did. Graeme Obree confounded sceptics and supporters alike when 24 hours after his failure he rode further in one hour than anybody had done before, covering 51.596 kilometres, a 445-metre improvement on Moser's figures. Chris put on a brave face to the journalists' questions, saying that it would not affect his plans, and joking that Obree should enjoy the record while he could for the next six days.

But underneath the public posturing, Chris admits: 'I was devastated. It meant that I wasn't going for the record of a legend. I was going for the record of a bloke from Scotland who made his own bikes. It wasn't quite the same.' Boardman had hit a setback and Keen shared the disappointment: 'I felt cheated in the way that Chris did, but I was convinced that he would get it.'

In the days after Obree's success, Chris's form – that hard-to-define feeling of well-being and guide to a rider's level of fitness – took a sudden dip. Perhaps it was the psychological blow that Obree had delivered, or the cumulative effect of the months of preparation, combined with his close

In complete contrast to the shadow-like Lotus, the French-built Corima hour record bike was curvaceous and bold. It was also very rigid and very light – weighing only 16 ½lbs. Originally designed as a sprint machine, the Corima featured 'outriggers' custom-built for Chris.

After a light breakfast, he rode through the five miles of rolling countryside to the velodrome with Paul Jennings. They arrived in the track centre by 8:30am and already people were milling around, drawn by Boardman's world class sideshow to the Tour de France. Peter Woodworth had been prepared for a big crowd and a large press turn-out and had requested a security team from the stadium owners. The six burly minders proved useful in holding back 100 or so journalists and photographers when Chris appeared.

In the changing rooms beneath the track centre Chris was focusing his thoughts on the task in front of him. 'I was prepared to make it the most unpleasant experience I'd ever had,' he says. 'It's not possible to ride absolutely flat out for that long, so you aim to ride at threshold and I knew what that would feel like.'

Threshold is the level just below the rider's absolute maximum. Every fibre of every muscle – shoulders, arms, neck, fingers as well as legs – is screaming at you to stop. You feel you can't hold on another second, and yet you have to continue with this pain for 60 minutes, of which each

involvement in the organization of the record attempt. Whatever the reason, he would have to go for the record on the scheduled date. There were no alternatives. 'It was the 23rd, the day that the Tour de France was in town, or we didn't do it at all,' says Peter Woodworth.

Chris was awake at 6:30am on Friday 23 July.

Just minutes before the hour record attempt, Peter Woodworth and Paul Jennings look on anxiously as Peter Keen sprays Chris with ethyl alcohol to combat the high indoor heat and humidity at Bordeaux's Lac velodrome.

second seems an eternity. In addition, there's the psychological difficulty of concentrating on riding round that track so many times. For anyone racing at this intensity the track is a desperately lonely place, despite an audience of thousands – that's why this record is so formidable and why so many are discouraged from even attempting it.

The Corima bike was given a last-minute checkover by UCI officials to make sure it was race legal and then it was time to face the crowd waiting to witness a piece of cycling history. A Granada TV film crew had also been following Chris's progress as he prepared for the record and they were right behind him as he entered the stadium to huge acclaim from nearly three thousand people.

Peter Keen remembers this moment: 'We walked in, followed by TV cameras. It was like a boxing match. The crowd reaction when they saw him was amazing. I thought 'this is showtime, we can't afford to lose'.' Surrounded by these pressures, Boardman as always appeared outwardly calm. Inside he was preparing himself for a performance unlike anything else he had done. Despite his experience of racing at the highest level, nothing could prepare him for this – not even the Olympic final. 'At the Olympics if it had gone wrong I would still have had the silver medal. With the hour you either do it or you fail.'

The weather, high air pressure and temperature and 80 percent humidity, would cause problems for Chris, and according to Keen, would mean that the attempt would take place in conditions equivalent to 200 metres below sea level. The stadium owners' insistence on switching on the powerful arc lights for the benefit of the TV cameras did not help, as the temperature rose even higher. After a preliminary warm-up ride it was decided to spray Chris with ethyl alcohol, which would evaporate and cool his skin, at least for a short while.

It was obvious that the crowd were ready and waiting for a show. 'They cheered when I came into the track, when I put on my helmet, when I got on the bike. It was great – really good support,' says Chris. Sitting in his trackside cabin, hidden from the eyes of the crowd but not from the press, he took a few last moments to gather himself for the task ahead.

After a final warm up it was time to report to the officials waiting on the start line. In the past, every time he had raced at international level the BCF had undertaken all the organization and planning. At Bordeaux, all the decisions were down to Chris and his team. As he waited on the start line there was another decision – the final one – to make. In the hour record, the rider decides when he will start. 'The guy just said "go when you're ready". That's the hardest thing in the world to do, because it's usually decided for you.'

In those final few minutes a hush fell over the stadium, all eyes focused on the yellow and red clad figure on the start line, the silence broken only by the excited voice of a Colombian reporter making a live broadcast to listeners 4,000 miles away. Chris could hear him too, but was unperturbed. 'I was sitting there, saying to myself "you've got to go now. Come on, you've got to go now" and I could hear everyone saying "ssshhh" to this guy. I felt like saying "no, you're alright, carry on".'

At two minutes past ten Chris Boardman launched himself forward into that unknown hour. The once-silent crowd erupted into a roar of encouragement, a noise that would increase in volume as it became clear that they were watching cycling history being made.

Standing in the back straight monitoring Chris's progress, Peter Keen was finally realizing his dream: he had prepared a rider for the hour record. Now all that remained to be seen was whether that rider would succeed. Everything in training suggested that he would. He had unoffi-

Critical countdown – his shoulders bowed under the pressure of the impending ordeal, Chris waits for the right moment for the 'off', gathering his thoughts as the press crowd in.

He's up! Split times on the electronic display showed Chris ahead of Obree at every 5 kilometre split from 10 kilometres onwards.

cially broken three world records in the previous four weeks. But this was the real thing. Despite the fact that Chris was on target from the early laps, Keen knew that it was not a foregone conclusion that he would do it. 'Others had started equally well, only to fade before half distance,' he says. But Chris Boardman did not fade. After the first comparison with Obree's record at 5 kilometres, when he was slower than the Scot, Chris moved ahead. At each 5 kilometres check he was faster, the roar of the crowd underlining this as they reacted to the times displayed on the electronic scoreboard.

Chris was racing around the smooth timber boards at a point just below his maximum level and was beginning to feel the effects of the heat building up in the stadium. 'I was starting to get light-headed and was worried about passing out,' he said. 'I didn't want to push it so far that I fainted, and in that heat it was a possibility.' His wife Sally, watching with friends in the home straight, could see that he was suffering: 'He kept going wide on the corners. You could see he was dizzy because it was affecting his riding.'

However, from being one second behind Obree at the 5-kilometre point, Chris moved two seconds clear at 10 kilometres; but his time of 11 minutes, 30.844 seconds was slower than his schedule – a series of lap-time strategies devised by Keen to help the rider pace his race and which

*His face drawn and pale and bathed in sweat, Chris faces
the world's press who descended en masse direct from the
Tour de France after his record 52.270 kilometres. Peter
Woodworth (right) attempts to hold back the mob.*

aimed at 52.5 kilometres for the hour. As he fell behind Keen simply moved to the next schedule – one of several plans they had prepared for the event – this one for 52.4 kilometres, still on target to beat the record although with a smaller margin.

At 30 kilometres, Chris had been riding for 34 minutes, 25.545 seconds – 25 seconds faster than Obree, and nearly two minutes faster than the legendary Eddy Merckx had been at the same point in 1972.

There were many British supporters in the crowd, including a group from Chris's North Wirral Velo club, and Bill Warren, operations director of Kodak Prints, the team's sponsor. Warren was overwhelmed by what he saw in the Bordeaux velodrome, and claims that this was not entirely due to his commercial interest in the man hurtling around the track, but more to do with the intensity of the spectacle. 'I've seen Liverpool win the European Cup, I've watched the All Blacks against England, and I've seen lots of other top level sports,' he says 'but I've never seen anything that compared to that hour record.'

Alan Dunn was also there to watch Chris's attempt. He had watched Moser's record nine years earlier, so this attendance made him unique: 'We were in Mexico while the band made a video so I went along to see Moser,' says Alan. 'Mick came too. He'd seen some racing before so it wasn't new to him.'

Twelve months earlier Boardman had relentlessly pursued Jens Lehmann in the Olympic final, catching and eliminating his rival. Now he was just as relentless as he hunted down Obree's record, the 40 kilometres time on the scoreboard showing that he was 53 seconds ahead of the Scot. According to these figures, if the two had started this ride together Chris would by now be three laps in front of Obree.

Although he was suffering, eyes staring fixedly ahead, his mouth open wide in an attempt to draw in oxygen from the hot, cloying atmosphere, he was aware of what was happening around him, and he knew that there was not much longer to go. 'Getting to half distance was the worst part of it. The last ten kilometres was great, and the last five, when I knew I had it, was just an ego trip.'

At 50 kilometres he was still ahead of Obree, and 72 seconds faster than Moser had been at the same point. Chris now had less than three minutes to go before his hour was up. He knew it was nearly over, but when the pistol shot rang out to signal the end of 60 minutes, he carried on. 'I didn't hear the gun because of the crowd – I couldn't hear a thing,' said Chris. 'It was only when I saw Peter Keen and Paul Jennings leaping up and down that I realized it was over.'

The 'hour', Chris Boardman's 'hour', was over. He had ridden further than anybody had before in the 100 years that racing cyclists have used 60 minutes' unaided riding as the ultimate challenge. He had covered 52.270 kilometres; 674 metres further than Obree and more than a kilometre in front of Moser's 1984 distance.

He and Keen had planned four or five laps 'warming down' to avoid a sudden stop after the intense effort. He didn't get the chance as reporters and TV crews swarmed onto the track, at one point nearly forcing the Olympic champion and world hour record holder from his bicycle.

Peter Woodworth was waiting in the home straight when Boardman came to a halt, putting his arms around the shoulders of the man who had put the record attempt together. Not many words passed between the two, but Woodworth knew what Chris was feeling: 'It was a really intense feeling of relief that it was over and he'd done it – not so much for himself, but for everyone else.'

As a publicity stunt, the hour record was timed to perfection. With the Tour de France due to arrive in Bordeaux later the same day – the outcome already settled – the press were hungry for fresh copy, and Chris and his team obliged with a world-shattering cycling story.

Engulfed by the scrum of journalists, Chris tried to answer the barrage of questions being fired at him, ranging from the obvious 'how do you feel?' to the surreal 'what do you think of Colombian cyclists?' from the South American reporter who had been so vociferous as Chris started.

The crowd parted with a 'Madame Boardman!' as Sally made her way through to embrace her husband, to much sympathetic 'aahing' from the onlookers. The electronic scoreboard reminded everyone of what they had just witnessed: 'Record du Monde Battu: 52.270 kilometres '.

Part one of the show was over. Part two would take place later that afternoon, following the finish of the Tour de France stage. The plan to show the world what Chris Boardman was capable of had worked. Later that day he would once again be in the spotlight when he shared the podium with Miguel Indurain, the Tour de France leader.

As Chris waited in the VIP enclosure as the Bordeaux stage finished, several of the riders came over to congratulate him as soon as they crossed the line. They had been told en route of his progress by their team managers, who had listened to the live radio coverage. This underlines the power of the hour. The plan had worked. Chris Boardman had taken the world hour record in a blaze of publicity, under the noses of the most influential people in the world of professional cycle racing. But before he would look at the professional opportunities that must now surely come his way, there was one more amateur goal to achieve.

CHAPTER SIX

Duel in the Ring

THE CELEBRATIONS FOR THE HOUR RECORD did not last long. Two days after riding further in one hour than anybody had done before, Chris returned to the Bordeaux velodrome to begin training for his next target, the world championship 4,000 metre pursuit race in Hamar, Norway, which for the first time in its history was an open race for amateurs and professionals alike.

The championships would begin in less than four weeks' time. It wasn't just for training purposes that Boardman and Peter Woodworth stayed on in Bordeaux. Chris would take this chance to sit down and plan out his immediate future. 'It was something that he didn't do after Barcelona and he should have,' says Woodworth, who had begun to take on a more managerial role in Boardman's career. During Chris's stay at the hotel that had been his home for the previous three weeks, several interested parties from professional teams made contact with him, including Roger Legeay, the manager of the team sponsored by the French insurance company, GAN, whose riders include Tour de France triple-winner Greg LeMond. Legeay, himself a successful ex-pro racing cyclist, as well as many other managers were impressed, not only by Chris's performance in taking the hour record, but by the manner in which he did it, in the full glare of the media spotlight, making a show of cycle racing's 'blue riband' event *and* putting a Tour de France stage temporarily in the shade!

It was not only the team managers who were impressed by the show in Bordeaux. Bernard Hinault, five times Tour de France winner, compared Chris to Merckx and Moser, before adding that he thought that only the triple Tour de France winner, Miguel Indurain, could beat the new figure.

Miguel Indurain, the man tipped by many to be the most likely candidate to attempt the hour was himself non-committal, merely saying that he had doubted whether Chris could do it, but congratulating him on doing so.

Boardman is honest about the chances of his record surviving an attack from Indurain, and his awe of the hour record's history remains: 'I think the credibility of the hour has suffered since Graeme and I broke it,' he says, citing the long list of world class riders who have held it. 'If

ABOVE: *Tour de France winner Miguel Indurain is widely tipped as the man to break Chris's hour record.*

OPPOSITE: *Although the bronze medal at the 1993 pursuit championship was a personal disappointment for Chris, it showed prospective employers that he was a consistent top-level performer.*

someone like Indurain took it, the hour would get its value back.'

Moser, the man who had seen his decade-old record beaten twice in six days by a Scot and a Brit, was a little more reserved with his praise, suggesting that it was due to technological advances that his record was no more. The fact that the Italian had plans to make another attempt on the record, despite having officially retired in 1988, may have had something to do with this.

Chris had now decided that he had no other option but to turn professional. If he remained amateur or raced as a professional in Britain, 1994 would mean more of the same as he had been doing for years. He had raced in the National championships at Leicester every year since 1984, had won more than 30 British titles, and had ridden faster over 25 miles than anyone in the country. It would be nice to continue winning races like this, but a 'big fish, little pool' career did not appeal to him. So 1993 would be his last year as an amateur rider.

Despite this, he was still hesitant about committing himself to a continental career based in Belgium or France. There had been talk of him moving to America to take advantage of the racing there and he spoke with some US-based riders about this option. Sally had spent much of her childhood in Canada and the prospect of a North American lifestyle would have been more attractive than living in Ghent or Roubaix (the usual lot of a British rider's wife whose husband is intent on a pro career in Europe).

There were other reasons for his hesitation in moving to continental Europe: Chris was worried about the difficulty of moving the family to a country where they didn't speak the language and not least about the racing and in particular the 'overload' factor. First year professionals are often

thrown into too many long, hard races which can effectively finish them off after one season. He didn't want to ride the severe early season races of March and April, such as Het Volk and Paris-Roubaix – races of around 160 miles which are fought out over the unforgiving Flanders Plain, usually in harsh weather. Chris wanted to ease his way into the pro scene.

Peter Woodworth, however, convinced Chris that the American option was out, and that it had to be Europe. Woodworth believed that if Chris went to America the chance of real progress would be lost. 'I asked him whether he would be interested in signing a contract that would allow him some autonomy in choosing when and where he raced, and which would allow him to commute from home instead of living abroad' says Woodworth. 'He said that he'd think about going for that kind of option.'

Two days later Chris phoned Woodworth to say that if it could be arranged, he would be interested in a deal that would allow him that kind of independence. The next step was to find a suitable team that would pay Chris what he felt he was worth, and at the same time accept these provisos.

Woodworth listed the managers who had contacted Chris after Bordeaux. 'I phoned Roger Legeay and we arranged a meeting in Cardiff,' he says. Legeay would be in the Welsh capital in the middle of August with a five-man GAN team riding the Tour of Britain.

These arrangements made, Chris continued with his preparation. But in contrast to the dedicated and single-minded approach to training he had put in for Barcelona 12 months earlier, Boardman's training for the championships in Norway was patchy and spasmodic – a combination of a temporary loss of motivation and the travel involved in getting to these races.

From the euphoria and celebration of Bordeaux Chris returned to Britain, arriving at 3am on the day of the British team pursuit championship at Leicester. After snatching a few hours' sleep he drove from Hoylake to the Saffron Lane Stadium, and with the North Wirral Velo team of Paul Jennings, Simon Lillistone and Jon Walshaw, won the championship, beating the previous track record for this event, set by a Soviet Union team in 1982.

After the high-pressure atmosphere of Bordeaux, with the world's press hanging on his every word and TV cameras watching his every move, Chris found it difficult to motivate himself at Leicester, and it was only through not wanting to let his team-mates down that he managed to do so. But there was another reason for his 'distant' feeling: 'It was such a relief when the hour ride was over that I just switched off for a while,' he says.

On 7 August Chris flew to Newtownards in Northern Ireland to ride the 25-mile Champion of Champions race, moved from its usual date in May, where he would meet Graeme Obree for the first time since taking the hour record from him. Obree claimed that he had not been too disappointed, despite losing the most coveted of all cycling records to Chris after just six days: 'I expected him to get it. My ride wasn't as good as it could have been because it was only 24 hours

To avoid pulling his foot out in the violent effort of a pursuit start, as happened at the national championships in Leceister earlier that year, Obree cemented his shoes directly to the pedals prior to the 1993 world championships.

after my first attempt,' he says. Nevertheless, the arrival of the two hottest 'hour' properties in world cycling would draw the crowds in to see a showdown.

After an interview on Ulster Television, the two rode an exhibition pursuit race around the streets of Newtownards, but Obree crashed, cheating the crowd of a close battle with Chris. The following day brought cold, wet conditions for the 25 mile race. Once again, Obree's misfortune meant that a clear result could not be gained, as the Scot crashed on his way to recording 51 minutes, 38 seconds. Chris finished in 49 minutes, 6 seconds, but whichever way round they finished, the large crowd at the finish enjoyed seeing two world hour beaters, past and present, at close quarters.

Twenty-four hours later, after the short flight from Belfast to Liverpool, Chris drove with Peter Woodworth to Cardiff for the meeting with Roger Legeay. 'We had a good discussion about 1994 – the kind of races I might ride, that kind of thing, and we arranged to meet after the world championships for further talks.' The next day he flew out to Norway. He already held the Olympic title; now he looked forward to a chance to take the world title, with its distinctive rainbow jersey, to add to his roll of honour. Before leaving he was optimistic about his chances in Norway, saying that he hoped to be the first rider to break the 4 minutes, 20 seconds barrier. However, when he arrived in Hamar and began training, Chris knew there was something wrong. 'I was absolutely worn out mentally, and physically I was jaded. The motivation wasn't there, and that made the task even more difficult.' The pressures of the previous nine months, in particular the last month in the run-up to Bordeaux, had finally caught up with him.

Before leaving he had told Sally that he felt unsure of the possible outcome. 'He said that he wanted to show a respectable performance, and by that he meant win a medal,' says Sally.

Chris told journalists that he could be sixth or first, he just didn't know, but his main concern was to show some continuity after the Olympics and the hour record. It was continuity that Roger Legeay would be looking for. The Olympic title would have alerted him to Chris's potential, the hour record would have underlined his class, and a good performance at the world championships would demonstrate his consistency – a vital element in the makeup of a professional racing cyclist. Chris would do everything he could to win, but if he didn't, he wanted at least to be on the podium.

The world pursuit championship of 1993 will be remembered as the series in which Graeme Obree shook off his 'amusing eccentric' tag. In the qualifying round the Scot finished second, behind the French rider Philippe Ermenault, who had arrived in Norway as the world record holder. Boardman qualified third fastest, and with Shaun Wallace, who had been selected by Lotus to ride the latest version of their bike, in fourth place, Britain would have three riders contesting the semi-finals.

British fans had been hoping for a Boardman-Obree final: an event pitting together the two men who had captured the imaginations of sports fans around the world. Obree, with his hour record and strange-looking machine, Boardman with his Olympic title and later, the hour record too. It would have been a grand final, but the rules of the knockout system meant that Ermenault, the fastest qualifier, would ride against Shaun Wallace and the Boardman-Obree clash would take place in the other semi-final.

Obree was psyched up, especially after Boardman had snatched Obree's one-week-old hour record, and wishes that it had been the final when they met: 'It was the crunch match. The last time I'd beaten him was at Newtownards, three years earlier,' Obree says. Despite meeting several

Obree was unbeatable during the 1993 world pursuit championship
series. The Scot set new world records in the semi-finals and the final,
silencing critics of the 'Obree position' for good.

times since then, he claims that this was his first chance to get even with Chris: 'I had to do it then – even my friends were beginning to say that I'd never beat him.' This was the incentive for Obree, who was thinking further ahead than the world championship. 'If I didn't beat him there, on the world stage, it would have been a blow to my career. It would have meant that me and my bike were not taken seriously.'

As the time for the semi-final approached, the two men prepared themselves, warming up their muscles for the effort ahead on bikes set up on rollers, just feet apart from each other. Although they would both be wearing the red, white and blue of Great Britain, once the race began national loyalties would be forgotten. It would be each rider for himself as they fought for a place in the final.

Chris had his back-up team of Peter Keen and Peter Woodworth to help him, which was just as well as this may have caused a problem for Doug Dailey, the British team manager, who was looking after the Scot. In the last few minutes he warned Obree against starting too fast, something which he tended to do. Dailey also told Obree about the system he would use to let him know how the Scot was doing against Boardman during the race: 'If I stand in front of the finish line, walking towards you, you're leading him,' Dailey told the pensive Obree. 'If I'm the other side of it, walking away, then he's leading you.'

Boardman and Obree lined up: Obree as the faster qualifier was in the home straight, while Boardman was opposite him, in the back straight. After the last-minute checkover by UCI officials, the starter's signal sent them on their way. Obree was behind Boardman for the first two laps as he struggled to build up momentum, but after that point Dailey's position was always before the finish line, walking towards Obree – the signal that he

was leading. Chris was slipping behind, his chances of adding the world championship to his Olympic title decreasing with each revolution of his pedals.

Despite his lead, the Scottish rider was having a communication breakdown over Dailey's track-side signals. 'I got confused and when I saw Doug walking towards me I thought it meant Chris was leading me,' says Obree. This explains why, with an already comfortable lead, Obree picked up the pace at the end of his ride. 'I wasn't trying to make Boardman look silly or anything, I thought that if I sprinted I might just get him back at the finish.'

Obree's 4 minutes, 22.668 seconds ride – a new world record – was his first defeat of Boardman in three years. But Chris was not complaining: the Hoylake rider's time of 4 minutes, 25.052 seconds was good enough for the bronze medal. He had ridden as fast as he had in Barcelona: 'I went there to do a reasonable ride after the hour and a bronze medal is exactly that,' he says. 'What amazes me about it is that I thought 'Oh yeah, a bronze medal' and put it in my pocket. Eighteen months earlier I'd have been elated with it.'

As the Scot stood at the trackside he shook his head in disbelief at setting a new world record: 'I can't believe it – I'm in the final,' was all he could manage to speak to Doug Dailey and Martin Coll, his manager. Boardman came to a halt alongside him. Shaking his hand, Chris congratulated Graeme, saying, 'Well done, mate – I wasn't going to beat that, not today.'

Obree went off to prepare himself for the following day's final against Ermenault while Chris went back to the hotel. He returned to loan Obree his aerodynamic helmet for the final – a sporting touch from a man who was, despite his brave face, disappointed with his defeat. 'At least something of mine will be in the world championship final,' he mused.

The next day, Chris watched from the track centre as Obree disposed of Philippe Ermenault, breaking his own day-old world record on his way to winning the championship. 'I felt pleased for Graeme. I knew what he would be feeling, winning the world championship,' says Chris. 'I was disappointed, but I couldn't have tried harder than I did. Graeme was the best in the world in 1993. He went faster in every round of the series – that's what impressed me.'

Chris had to pick himself up and look ahead. He had a world championship bronze medal and he was meeting Roger Legeay the following day to discuss a professional contract. He couldn't afford to be down for too long.

One of the factors that makes Chris Boardman the rider that he is is his ability to recover from a setback, something that has developed out of necessity over the years. It may appear that his career has flowed seamlessly from the talented 13 year-old to Olympic champion and world hour record holder, but it hasn't been quite like that. 'I've always had disappointments and upsets – they are part of racing,' he says. 'When I was 15, a lad named Lee Proctor always beat me. After him it was Guy Silvester, then Colin Sturgess. Now it's Graeme.'

He doesn't complain about the fact that there is always someone there to stop him from sweeping the board; he sees this as being beneficial to the sport, for spectators and for himself. 'When there is somebody else there it means you never get

British pursuiting reached an all-time high in 1993 when three of the top four riders were British. In the end a Frenchman, Philippe Ermenault (left), scuppered hopes of a clean sweep of the medals by taking silver. Graeme Obree (centre) took the gold with Chris gaining bronze.

complacent. You can't afford to. If they beat you, you want to turn that around, and if they are threatening to beat you, it's great motivation.

The next stage of Chris's career would mean that there would be many more than the occasional rider to challenge him.

CHAPTER SEVEN

Turning Pro

TO BE A PROFESSIONAL RIDER means starting at the bottom and working your way up. Eventually, if you are talented enough, you will be accepted by the top riders, who guard their positions in the professional hierarchy jealously. Chris did not imagine that he would start at the bottom of the pile. He knows his capabilities, and he knows his value.

In a three-hour meeting with Roger Legeay in his hotel room in Norway, Chris and Peter Woodworth discussed a contract for 1994. Legeay agreed that it would be unwise to put Chris through a severe programme in his first year, and a deal was reached which suited both parties. A better example of just how much influence the hour has in professional racing could not be found than in the relative ease with which Chris Boardman negotiated and secured such a contract. Legeay wanted a letter of assurance that Chris would ride for GAN in the following year, but Chris went one step further. He had planned to race in a series of international time trials in continental Europe, and a decision was made. 'I ended my amateur career in that hotel room,' says Chris. 'I was riding the Eddy Merckx Grand Prix and the Grand Prix des Nations in September anyway, so I agreed to ride them for GAN.'

Chris Boardman's decision to turn professional and ride the remainder of the 1993 season with GAN, the French insur-

ABOVE: *GAN team manager Roger Legeay made a special effort to draw up a contract for Chris which reflected his desire to commute to and from the UK.*

OPPOSITE: *Facing the future – on the start line on 1 September for his first race as a professional in the 1993 Eddy Merckx Grand Prix in Belgium.*

ance company, meant that he would remain under the spotlight of the world's cycling media. His first race would be the Eddy Merckx Grand Prix time trial in Brussels, where his performance would be analyzed closely by the media pundits, eager to see if Chris could live up to the reputation that his hour record had given him. If he had waited until February 1994 he could have entered the professional ranks in relative anonymity by beginning his career in the races held on the French Riviera which have become cycling's equivalent of football's pre-season friendly matches. These races allow new riders to blend in, hidden away in the 150-man field as they find their feet before the real racing begins in March.

In the Eddy Merckx Grand Prix time trial, alone and unaided against the clock, there would be no place to hide – no easy ride to the finish. Chris was well aware of this, and he felt that on his present form he would not be a contender for the honours in the Merckx race. Back at home in Hoylake, Chris Boardman began a training programme designed to bring him to the level of fitness that he had before the world championships. He also used this period to adjust himself to his new status as a professional. 'I felt a bit like I did when I moved out of my parents' house. It was the natural thing to do, but it took a bit of getting used to,' he says.

Chris trained on the roads of the Wirral and North Wales in the two weeks before the time trial in Brussels, sometimes alone, and sometimes with the mixed group of amateurs and professionals that he regularly trained with. As Chris Boardman and Peter Woodworth flew out to the Belgian capital on 10 September 1993 Chris was apprehensive about the race and everything surrounding it. 'I knew what a time trial was like – they're always the same. But it was the scale of it all that I found really daunting.' It is understandable that he felt like this. Even the title of this race is formidable.

Eddy Merckx, arguably the world's greatest ever rider, is involved with the organization of the 66-kilometre time trial that carries his name. Although it does not qualify for the world cup, the season-long series which decides the most consistent top performer of the year, the Eddy Merckx GP is a top-level race. Despite his recent training, Chris was not optimistic about his chances. There was something not quite right; something he could not quite put his finger on. His approach to the race had to be realistic: 'It was just for experience

Chris prepares for work before a stage of the 1994 Tour of the Mediterranean. Chris studied the opposition closely during these early season events and this was to prove invaluable as the season progressed.

really. I was prepared to finish well down the results sheet, but I wanted to do the best I could.'

The race consists of two 33-kilometre laps which thread their way through Brussels' northern suburbs. In cold, wet conditions, Chris started fourth from last in the 20-man field, two minutes in front of another rider who was also finding his way in this new life – Graeme Obree. Turning pro before Boardman, Obree did not compete with a team and did not have a single sponsor; in his maverick style he tended to make one-off deals for each race.

Roger Legeay, the GAN manager, was driving the team car behind Chris. In the event of a puncture or crash the car carries spare bikes and wheels and a change can be made in a matter of seconds. Peter Woodworth was with Legeay and so was able to watch the team manager's reaction to his new rider: During the first lap Chris hurtled downhill on narrow roads made treacherous by the rain, the chance of a crash present with every pedal stroke. After negotiating a slippery roundabout at speed and then immediately taking a sharp right-hand turn, leaning his bike over to the limit, the occupants of the car held their breath 'It looked as though he wasn't going to get round it. We thought he was going to hit the kerb,' recalls Woodworth.

'He got through it without a problem and Legeay turned to his mechanic in the passenger seat, raised an eyebrow, and nodded.' This was the first time the GAN manager had seen Chris Boardman racing on the road, and he was impressed by his riding skills. He was even more impressed after the first lap, when the result board showed that Chris was 34 seconds ahead of the field. As an amateur in 1991 Chris had won the prestigious GP de France time trial, so Boardman watchers abroad at least would have been aware of his potential in the time trial even before Barcelona brought him to the world's attention. But this was different. This was a professional time trial. Double world champion Gianni Bugno was riding, along with Jelle Nijdam a rider whose time trial expertise had brought him stage wins in the Tour de France. Chris's pure speed had made the transition from

the smooth timbered four kilometres of the velodrome to the rain-soaked, cold roads of Belgium.

Raising himself out of the saddle on the rises, his legs pumping the pedals to ensure that the high speed was maintained despite the gradient, Chris extended his lead, the crowd along the route roaring their encouragement at seeing the Olympic champion and hour record holder taking on and beating the established professionals.

While Chris was heading for victory, Graeme Obree was not having such a good race. He was riding a road version of his track bicycle similar to the one he used to great effect in British time trials; but at the end of the first lap he was in seventh place. Any chance that he had to improve on this over the remaining 33 kilometres were dashed when he lost control of his machine after hitting a drain and crashed into the crowd. Fortunately, for Obree at least, his fall was broken by a well-padded spectator, but his momentum was lost and he finished in 10th place.

However, it seems that even before Obree arrived in Brussels, all was not well. 'It was a total disaster. I was unprepared for it. I hadn't planned to be racing so late in the year and I hadn't been well, either,' says Graeme.

'But even if I hadn't crashed I wouldn't have beaten Chris.'

On the day, nobody could beat Chris Boardman. In a remarkable professional debut he had triumphed over a quality field. He was on the way to making up for the disappointment in Norway three weeks earlier. Standing by his team car afterwards, being interviewed by the press and signing autographs, Chris acted as though it was the most natural thing in the world, but this was not the result that he had been expecting. 'It was a real surprise when I won. I thought my form was only mediocre, and I was really only aiming at a

THE FASTEST MAN ON 2 WHEELS

placing.' Despite the list of riders behind Chris, he was aware that the top men in the world were not riding, and that those who were had ridden a hard season which included the three week-long Tour de France. 'I kept it in perspective,' he says. 'The real test would be the Grand Prix des Nations.'

The Grand Prix des Nations is the time trial that all professionals would like to have on their list of victories. The roll of honour of this race is as impressive as that of the hour record holders, and Chris was hoping to show well in the race that brings to an end the short elite time trial season for the professionals.

Despite the accident and 10th place in Brussels, Graeme Obree did not escape the attention of the crowd. Like Chris, he was surrounded by autograph hunters and journalists, with a shared curiosity about the Scotsman with the revolutionary ideas and bicycles. Eddy Merckx himself was impressed by the two Britons. While pointing out that Obree's bike was probably not suited to this race, the legendary Belgian told reporters: 'Boardman has taken his revenge for his defeat in Norway in the best possible manner.' Obree himself recognized this, but says that he was not upset by the result. 'I was pleased for Chris in the same way that he must have been pleased for me in the world championship semi-final.'

Chris returned home from Brussels to continue his training before flying out to his next race five days later, the Telekom GP at Baden Baden in Germany. This was a race where teams of two riders relay each other over the distance, one taking the lead while the other rests, taking shelter behind his partner. Chris was paired with Claudio Chiappucci, the Italian whose attacking style and buccaneering attitude has made him a Tour de France hero over the last three years.

The race would be decided over eight laps of a

9.2 kilometre circuit and the Italian star had told Chris the night before when they discussed their strategy to lead him on the early stages and he would try to share the pace when he could. As Chiappucci had predicted, he did have difficulty in the early stages but settled in before half-way, just as Chris hit a bad patch and began struggling to hold the pace. Boardman was having trouble adapting to the erratic riding style of his partner as the Italian rode up the hills in explosive bursts in contrast to Chris's steadier climbing style.

As Chris was beginning to recover and was able to share once again the work-load with Chiappucci, a problem with his bike meant that he had to stop and change to his spare machine. The spare bike did not have a bottle and in the high temperature Chris suffered even more in the final laps. It was a difficult ride: 'It was really ragged. We never got into a good steady pace because our styles were so different' says Chris. Despite this, he and Chiappucci finished second to Bugno and Fondriest, and for the second time in his two week professional career Chris was in the media spotlight as he shared the podium with the winners of the race and his partner.

One of the most pleasing aspects of Boardman's new pro career was the way that he was accepted by his fellow professionals. In the highly competitive world of pro bike racing a new challenger might expect a cool reception, particularly when he wins his first race, and especially when he has received as much media attention as Chris had. 'It was a pleasant surprise as the majority of them seem OK. The ones who have gone out of their way to be nice are Bugno Chiappucci and Fondriest' he says. He admits to getting a buzz from being with these riders. 'It really annoys me when it happens, but it does. At the Telekom race we were having breakfast and I was thinking "wow,

I'm sitting with Bugno and Chiappucci", but it stops as soon as the race begins.'

It was natural enough that he should feel like this. Chris had watched these men on TV and read about them for years, and now he was up there, not only riding with them, but actually competing for the top honours. 'I've climbed up the ladder and now I feel like I can see the top rung. Once you start riding with these guys, then you know you are a good bike rider.' said the man who was not only riding with them, but was making his presence felt amongst this elite.

Chris's next test would be the Duo Normand, seven days after the Telekom race. But first the Olympic champion had some work to do for the Manchester Olympic team bidding for their city to be the venue for the Games in the year 2000. As a British Olympic gold medallist – and the only one

Launching off the starting ramp with Italian partner Claudio Chiappucci during the Telekom 2-up, in September 1993. This was a tough race for Chris – Chiappucci made him suffer on the climbs and he had to change bikes after mechanical trouble.

in the north west of England – Chris had been contacted by the bid committee to join Linford Christie and other British medallists from Barcelona in a last minute lobbying trip to persuade the International Olympic Committee to vote for Manchester. He was more than happy to lend his support to Manchester's case but was bemused by what was only a last-minute decision to include some athletes in the final bid presentations. 'I think someone pointed out that it might look a bit strange if it was just the officials there and none of the competitors.' Chris flew to Monte

Carlo along with Sally for the announcement of the IOC's choice. In the end it didn't matter, as Sydney won the nomination. 'It was a pity. It would have been good for the country, particularly the North West.' says Chris.

Earlier in the evening, as they waited for the decision to be announced, the different countries entered into the spirit of things by singing the opening bars of their National Anthems. Sally jokingly asked an Australian sitting next to her if he and his compatriots would join the British contingent in 'God save our gracious Queen' when their turn came. ' When he said 'a minority might but the majority won't' I wondered what he was talking about ' said Sally. It was only later when she recognized him as Paul Keating, the Prime Minister of Australia and leading advocate of Aussie republicanism, that Sally realized the significance of his reply.

Chris may have been impressed by Manchester's bid but he was not so impressed with the protocol and attitudes that prevailed in the Mediterranean tax-free resort-principality of Monaco. 'We were invited out by some British ex-pats, to an evening function at a yacht club. I was wearing a shirt and tie but the receptionists at the club wouldn't let me in without a jacket.' Even an intervention from another Manchester team bidder, novelist Jeffrey Archer, couldn't sway things. 'He said "don't you know who this is? This is Chris Boardman, the Olympic gold medallist!" But this didn't work.' Eventually a jacket was borrowed and worn by Chris for the length of time it took to walk through the door to his table, and then immediately discarded. 'I know it's petty, but I was seething because these people had invited me and then tried to prevent me from coming in.'

At the end of the evening Chris and Sally shared a taxi back to their hotel with the former Conservative MP. 'When we arrived back we realized none of us had any money' says Chris, who was startled by Lord Archers' solution to the problem. 'He leaned out of the window and shouted to a hotel commissionaire "You! Give me some money for this taxi", as though it was the most natural thing to do. This time his powers of persuasion did work!'

From the sophistication of Monte Carlo the Boardmans flew home to Hoylake and reality. Chris had less than 24 hours before he flew to France for the Duo Normand and because of his trip to Monte Carlo he had been unable to train since his ride the previous Sunday with Chiappucci. The following day's time trial was another two-man race, over 52 kilometres against a mixed field of professional and amateur teams. Chris's enforced break didn't seem to affect his performance. In cold, wet conditions he and his team-mate from GAN, Laurent Bezault, won the race in 1 hour, 4 minutes, 26 seconds, just one second faster than two more GAN riders, Pascal Lance and Eddy Seigneur. In Chris Boardman's three-week professional career his record was first, second, first – an impressive record by any standards – but Chris knew that these races meant nothing when compared with the Grand Prix des Nations. A good performance in this classic time trial of the year would be the perfect end to his first pro season and a good foundation for 1994.

There was no need for Chris to fly anywhere the following weekend. He was riding a local invitation race, a hilly 32 miles round the roads of Delamere Forest in Cheshire. He had won this race on five previous occasions, and now his fans in and around Merseyside had their first chance to see him in his new GAN colours. On the day, Chris didn't feel 100 percent fit: 'My tests on the Kingcycle showed that I was well down on the power output level that I had for the hour record which was a bit worrying,' he says. But he wanted to win in front of his home crowd; and win he did. He considered this a fitting farewell to his English time trialling days. Chris knew there would be no more time to ride the races that have been the mainstay of his career since he was 13.

The following weekend Chris flew back to France to take part in the Chrono des Herbiers, a 48-kilometre time trial over the undulating roads on the outskirts of Nantes. He won the race by 59 seconds from his team mate, Pascal Lance. If the crowd were hoping to see a close battle between Chris and Graeme Obree, they were disappointed, as Graeme finished in fourth place, 2 minutes, 10 seconds behind Chris – his performance marred by a chest infection which had prevented him from training since the Eddy Merckx Grand Prix. Despite winning the race, all was not well with Chris. He was worried about his form and whether he would have the necessary fitness to win the GP des Nations, now just six days away.

The pressure was on too since the French press had named him as favourite for the race – based on his results in the autumn time trials and his status as world hour record holder. As he suspected, his fitness was not sufficient to take the victory. He finished fourth to Armand de las Cuevas, a rider tipped by team manager, Cyrille Guimard, as France's successor to the country's last Tour de France heroes, Hinault and Fignon. Fourth place in arguably the most famous time trial in the world was not enough to console Chris. 'I wanted a good performance in the Nations. I knew I was capable of winning it, so it was very disappointing,' he says 'When you are up against competition like that, you can't afford a bad day, and that's what happened to me'.

If Chris was disappointed with his fourth place, Graeme Obree would be even more upset as he finished in 15th position. He had also suffered an off-day, and looked forward to the Florence-Pistoia race seven days away, telling reporters that it was his last chance of redemption. If cycling fans were looking at these races as a duel between the two men, it had so far been a one sided duel. The time trial in Florence was the last of the year, so time was running out for the maverick Scottish rider.

Chris saw his experience in the GP des Nations as a positive one, despite his disappointment. Once again, his ability to pick himself up from a setback came into play: 'You have to accept that on some days you're just not good enough' Chris reflected, 'when you realize that, you're on the way to becoming a better rider.' He didn't have time to ponder over this latest result for too long because within hours he was on a flight to Venice for his next race, a one-kilometre time trial. Chris won this race, held the day after the GP des Nations, with Italy's new Hero, the world cup winner Maurizio Fondriest in second place.

There was one more time trial left on Chris's programme. After six days at home in Hoylake he flew once more to Italy for the Florence-Pistoia, where Fondriest turned the tables from the week before and relegated Chris to second place. In the eight races Chris had ridden with GAN since September 11 1993 his lowest placing had been fourth. He had stood on top of the winner's podium five times, and finished second twice – a convincing start to a pro career which riders, journalists, team managers and fans believed promised much more.

Ever since 1987, the year that Chris began working with Peter Keen, his preparation for the following year would always begin shortly after the last race of the current season – and 1993 was no exception. Together with Keen, he scheduled an autumn/winter training programme designed to bring him to fitness by March 1994 – the month in which the continental European season really gets underway. A measure of just how committed Chris was to his new career can be taken from the many lucrative offers from the organizers of the indoor winter track meetings that he turned down. He could have spent the months between October and March travelling throughout Europe earning money for brief appearances in exhibition races, or in 'revenge matches' with Obree. 'I wasn't going to compromise 1994 by racing all over the place all winter. I needed to be mentally fresh as well as physically fit.'

His training at home consisted mainly of Peter Keen's Level 2 sessions, some alone, and some with a group. With the longer distances that pro racing entails, some of these training rides in North Wales were increased to five hours, but generally his winter was spent as it had always been; seeing more of his family (with an addition on the way), socialising with friends, and mentally and physically preparing for the fresh challenges that the new year would bring.

Although he was wary of jeopardizing 1994 for the sake of appearance money, he did accept two invitations to race at the six-day races in Geneva and Bordeaux – big off-season attractions for cycling fans with a sprinkling of cycling stars from the road events. As its name suggests, a six-day race is run over six days and consists of different disciplines of track racing, from Madison (where the riders take turns in the race, relaying each other at high speed with hand slings), to motor-paced racing, in which a souped-up moped leads the individual riders, the purpose being to stay close behind your moped as it increases speed

Despite their rivalry, Chris and Obree (seated) *have a healthy respect for each other. They are pictured here chatting at the Bordeaux six-day race in November 1993.*

until your rivals are left behind. There are some who feel that the six days have as much in common with professional bike racing as televised wrestling does with its Olympic cousin, but they are a tremendously popular form of sporting entertainment, particularly in continental Europe. A band plays in the track centre, alongside the restaurant, which gives diners a ringside view of the racing.

The organizers of these races promised the crowds a Boardman-Obree revenge match. The possibility of a showdown between Boardman and Obree would be the draw the organizers needed to get the crowds in during the relatively quiet early nights of the competition, and the two certainly provided some exciting racing. At the six-day meeting at Bordeaux there would be three events in which Obree and Boardman would compete. The Revenge Match was to be held over two 4-kilometre pursuit races followed by a 10-kilometre pursuit race. Boardman won the first two, but was caught before half distance by Obree in the final race. 'When Graeme wants to make a point, he really makes it,' says Chris. The Scot won the series, so helping to erase the memory of the Eddy Merckx GP and Grand Prix de Nations.

In December 1993, *Cycling Weekly* magazine drew up a list of the Boardman-Obree meetings, including time trials and track races, that had taken place during that year: the result was 11-3 in Chris's favour, but now the two riders and their fans would have to wait until 1994 to see if the rivalry would continue and how it would be resolved.

Chris's decision to go to Bordeaux was also influenced by the fact that GAN's head office is in the city and Chris had to attend a meeting there with the rest of the 20-strong squad. He and Peter Keen wanted to use the velodrome to evaluate the

differences between various bikes, ranging from a conventional track machine to the Corima bike used by Chris in the hour record, and an Obree-type bicycle. Together with Peter Woodworth, they carried out these tests during the periods when there was no racing at the track, in an attempt to find out if Obree's position did offer a significant improvement in performance. Shortly after the tests, the UCI stated that 'the Obree position' had been banned from use on the road, and was under review for track use. Chris was pleased that this happened: 'I didn't want to use Graeme's position, but if I had to I would have done' he says. 'The UCI had taken it out of my hands...' Chris believes that although he himself was connected with a major technological development in cycle racing through the Lotus bike, things are going too far in this direction. The decision of the UCI may signal a return to more conventional types of bicycles, which is something that Chris welcomes. 'It would mean that the rider becomes the focus again, and not the bike, which has been the case in the last two years.'

At the team meeting in Bordeaux Chris met his new team-mate Greg LeMond for the first time. The American is nearing the end of a turbulent career that has seen him win three Tours de France and the world championship road race, despite being shot in a hunting accident in 1987, the year after his first Tour victory. LeMond came close to death following the shooting, but fought his way back to fitness, winning the Tour de France in 1989 and 1990. 'We got on well when we met,' says Chris. 'I admire him for questioning the norms in pro cycling and all the things that people had been doing for years. If it was valid he'd respect it, but if it was just tradition for tradition's sake, he'd challenge it.'

Boardman and other top riders of today

acknowledge LeMond as the rider who dragged cycling out of the days when professionals were often paid a pittance. LeMond negotiated the first million-dollar contract and the knock-on effect has been felt by most riders who earn their living through bike racing – even though potential earnings are not in the same league as tennis, football and many other sports.

Just before Chris left Bordeaux details were taken of his height and dimensions so that his team bikes could be prepared for the following season. Although he had finished the 1993 season wearing GAN colours he had been riding a Cougar machine instead of the team issue 'Greg LeMond' bike. This had been agreed with Legeay before Chris signed his contract. 'I wanted to do that for the people at Cougar, who have helped me over

Boardman goes before Bugno! Chris signs on before a stage of the 1994 Tour of the Mediterranean while double world champion Gianni Bugno waits his turn. After the initial thrill of riding alongside some of his heroes Chris soon settled in to the pro peloton.

the years,' he says.

It was a substantial thank-you, as the name of Cougar, the Liverpool based bicycle frame manufacturer was seen around the world due to the press and TV coverage that Chris received during that triumphant autumn.

In the middle of November, with his racing and team duties over for the year, Chris, Sally and the children flew to America for a long-overdue holiday at Mammoth Mountain, California. It was their first holiday since they were 17, and Chris's parents, Keith and Carol, went too as a present from the couple for their support over the year. Chris had intended to do some skiing but the possibility of injury put him off the idea. Instead he and the family relaxed amid the wonderful scenery. At 9000 feet, the high altitude took some getting used to, even for an Olympic champion. 'I pulled Edward on a sledge up one of the slopes so he could sledge down it,' says Chris. 'I could hardly breathe when we reached the top. But the snow was so powdery we sank into it and I had to pull him all the way down too.'

Recharged by the break, Chris returned home to put the final touches to his pre-Christmas preparation. In January the serious training began for a year that would pitch him against the world's best. In the early part of the month, keeping to Peter Keen's Level 2 training programme, he pedalled the roads of Wirral and North Wales, before flying out to Bordeaux to meet the rest of the GAN team for a week of training.

The professional teams of continental Europe have not yet accepted the value of the Peter Keen's coaching ideas, so the week with GAN would mean that Chris would be riding for four to five hours a day, for six days. This had worried him before he left for France. 'It was a completely new departure for me, nothing like the training I do, so I was a bit concerned about how I'd fit into it. The distances worried me too.' For someone whose speciality is riding at maximum over much shorter distances, and whose training programme is tailored to allow rest days after any long rides, it is understandable why Chris had these doubts, but as these extracts from his own diary show, it wasn't as bad as he thought it would be:

Tuesday, 25 January

It seemed as though I'd been asleep for five minutes when the alarm went off at 8am. This felt like my first real day as a pro. I was nervous because we had to do 190 kilometres, but it went so well that 5 hours later I felt fine. I even had time to appreciate the scenery, which is superb. I'm usually oblivious to that kind of thing!

Wednesday, 26 January

After some team photos had been taken, we left at 9.30 for a 180 kilometre loop. It was hideously windy, so I spent a lot of time trying to shelter in the group. One of the team, Herve Garel, decided to give me a hard time in the crosswind, forcing the pace up a bit at a time. If I'd responded to him we would have ended up riding at Mach Two, but he cracked after a while and I avoided him after that.

Thursday, 27 January

It must be getting to me – I had some really bizarre dreams last night so I was glad to wake up. Another 180 kilometres today, and up to 150 kilo-

Lining up for the first stage of a team time trial, Chris is the only rider without tri-bars yet he proved to be one of the strongest in the team, which dropped three of its eight before the finish of the 1994 Tour of the Mediterranean.

metres I was going reasonably well. The last hour was tough, so I appreciated my massage tonight, even though a TV crew were filming me. The masseur decided to have a laugh at their expense and started grinding his teeth noisily as he bent my leg at the knee. The camera-man zoomed in thinking that was where the noise was coming from!

Friday, 28 January

Heavy rain this morning. I got all my wet gear out, so of course the rain stopped and the sun came out instead. I saw more fantastic countryside, so it's now officially the most beautiful place I've ever visited. It was supposed to be a recuperation day, but I've never done nearly five hours on a rest day before. At dinner tonight I found to my horror that

Roger [Legeay] wasn't joking when he told me about the initiation rites for new team members. It wasn't buying the drinks that worried me (although as there were 30 of us, perhaps it should have done) – it was the singing. The new boys had to sing a song after buying the beer, and when it came to my turn I found myself singing two verses of Frere Jacques. Let me just say that you won't see me on *Stars In Their Eyes*, but it was a good laugh, and part of the team bonding.

Saturday, 29 January

Everyone looked tired at breakfast, and my legs could now be labelled as 'sore'. It was clear and sunny today, and I'll remember it as the best day I've ever had on a bike. As training it was less than intensive, but for great weather, a comfortable pace and the best scenery ever, it was something else. Chateau Biron was beautiful – really tranquil. I'd like to bring Sally and the kids here one day.

I had a short chat with Roger Legeay in the evening. He was happy with the way things are going, so I felt quite good about that. Later on the team had their traditional drinking ritual, involving half-litre cocktails of liqueurs, spirits and champagne. The inevitable conclusion came too soon for one of us; he didn't make it outside so the bread basket was utilized. Of course, I was in bed for 10pm, thinking ahead to the following day's ride, 180 kilometres and the last of the week.

It was a great six days for me – very different from my usual training, and useful because it gave me, apart from anything else, some idea of what it's like to ride for five or six hours every day for a week.

Chris would find out soon enough what it was like to race for that length of time. After a week at home, he flew back to France, this time to Montpellier, to begin his first race, the five day Tour of the Mediterranean. The first stage was a team time trial over 20 kilometres where GAN finished ninth, 36 seconds behind the winners, the Italian-Belgian GB-MG team. This powerful team is jointly sponsored by an Italian jeans manufacturer, MG and a Belgian supermarket chain, GB.

Cycle racing sponsorship is by no means restricted to the cycle trade. Chris's team is sponsored by GAN one of the biggest insurance companies in France, while the team of Miguel Indurain, the triple Tour de France winner is funded by Banesto, a Spanish bank. Spain's equivalent of the RNIB, *ONCE*, also sponsor a team, recognized as one of the strongest in Europe. There have been some strange cycling sponsors from many different businesses over the years. In the 1960s a team of Belgians who earned their living in one of the toughest sports in the world were sponsored by Romeo, a monthly magazine filled with Barbara Cartland-esque romantic love stories, while in 1973 another Belgian team were backed by Ketting Didam, the makers of ornamental coal scuttles.

Of course all of these companies have one thing in common: a desire to see their name on the television screens and in the newspapers as their riders compete in the races all over Europe. Obviously the best way to do this is for the riders to win the races, but even a failed attempt to win can mean two or three hours coverage on prime time television as the cameras focus on the rider with his sponsor's name emblazoned on his jersey and shorts. This is the reason why you will often see a rider who has no real chance of winning, make a move early on in a race to ensure that his bosses are pleased at the end of the day.

The second stage of the Tour of the Mediterranean took place on the afternoon of the team time trial and was a 99-kilometre stage from

Beziers to Lattes. With 200 riders, and in strong cross-winds, this stage came as a culture shock for Chris. Many of the riders were nervous as this was the first significant stage race of the year, and this, combined with the cross-wind and narrow roads, meant that there were lots of minor crashes. Chris was unsettled by all of this until he spoke to Scottish pro cyclist Robert Millar. The experienced Scot's advice, based on 14 years professional racing, helped him out. 'Robert came alongside me in the race and told me not to worry, that it was always like this in the early races. I felt better after that.' With five kilometres to go, Chris became a victim of one of the many crashes of the day, but was soon up and away again with just a few grazes on his knee to show for it, and he finished in the main group of riders. Chris was surprised at some of the reports that he read about his performance in this race. 'It was a training race as far as I was concerned. When it was obvious that I wasn't going to win a stage I would just ride it for training.'

The professional cyclists' year is a long one, from February to October, and it was perhaps a little unrealistic of some journalists to expect Chris to come out, racing at the limit, from the beginning of the year. He was playing by a new set of rules now, but he knew that when the time was right for him, he would prove himself. After finishing stage 6, 100 kilometres from Le Cannet to Hyeres, Chris decided to take his chance in the short afternoon stage, a 36-kilometre dash from Hyeres to the summit of Mont Faron. A stage of this length would be sure to have action as soon as it started, and Chris positioned himself at the front with a bunch of riders as they rolled out of Hyeres, their thoughts on the gruelling climb that awaited them less than an hour's ride away.

The expected attack came from two riders, Frederic Moncassin and Jean Pierre Heynderickx, and Chris was quick to join them. The three worked together to try and hold off the powerful GB-MG team who were organising the chase behind, building up a 36 second lead at one point, before eventually being pulled back. Although Chris finished the stage in 85th place, he was pleased with his 18 kilometres of freedom. 'I'd put my toe in the water and I could see what it was like after that stage, but I was glad to get GAN's name at the front as well.' he says.

Encouraged by this, he rode more aggressively

As the seven-day Tour of the Mediterranean progressed, Chris became more confident and by the end of the race his aggressive riding earned him the respect and praise of his fellow professionals.

on the following day's final stage. Attacking at different points he was always brought back by GB-MG, who were protecting their rider, Davide Cassani, the overall race leader. They did not want to take a chance and allow Boardman too much leeway, even though at this point he could not challenge Cassani's lead. 'I might have got away with it, but I came into this race with a reputation that I hadn't yet earned. I had a name but hadn't yet run a race, so I was marked.'

Chris finished the Tour of the Mediterranean in 65th place, behind the winner, Davide Cassani of GB MG. Each rider is timed every day, and the total riding time is calculated. Cassani's total time for the 730 kilometres was 17 hours, 33 minutes, 47 seconds; 13 minutes ahead of Chris. This was a good steady start to his pro career.

His next race would take him back to Monte Carlo, but this time he would not be worrying about the dress code at the Yacht Club. The Monte Carlo-Alassio race saw him finish in the bunch after a breakaway attempt with Evgeni Berzin, winner of the world pursuit championship in Japan in 1990. 'I broke clear with 20 kilometres to go, and Berzin came across to me. I couldn't stay with him on a climb, and lost contact.'

Once again Chris had been in a position to see what it was like out there: 'I could see the possibilities of what I could do.'

He must have been impressing the other riders because Adriano Baffi, the winner of Monte Carlo-Alassio and many other early season races, looked for him at the end to congratulate him.

Next was the Tour du Haut Var, a tough 160 kilometre race. After 60 kilometres a steep climb broke the race up. 'I was caught at the wrong end of the bunch and had to watch the break go.'

Chris was disappointed but kept up near the front of the race for the next three hours, finishing

16th out of 38 finishers, all that was left of a 160-man field. 'I was pleased with that, and so was Roger Legeay. You don't have to convince the world you're good – just convince the boss. He's the one who's paying you.'

Chris had 10 days at home before his next major race, the Tour of Murcia, another five day stage race. Roger Legeay had originally intended to put Chris in the Paris-Nice race, until the organizers cancelled the time trial stages of that race. Murcia was an ideal substitute as it had the time trial stages in which Chris would be expected to show, and the day before it started there was another race at Almeria, which would be a good warm-up.

Chris noticed that his form had dipped and thought it was perhaps a virus, but by the time he flew to Almeria he felt fine. 'It was as though someone had flicked a switch. I think it was fatigue after the Haut Var – I didn't realize at the time how much it had taken out of me.'

Gilbert Duclos-Lassalle, the veteran French rider on the GAN team, had said that this year's Haut Var was the hardest he'd ridden, so it seems that Chris had underestimated the effect it would have on him.

On 5 March Chris flew to Almeria. During a transfer his suitcase was lost. 'I learned the number one lesson for bike riders that day – always carry your racing shoes in your hand luggage.'

The team can supply spares of everything else: jerseys, shorts, helmets, bikes, but as Chris found out, they do not keep spare shoes. He borrowed a pair from Greg LeMond, customized by the American, and though they fitted Chris, they were uncomfortable to ride in. Another pair was found, but after 60 kilometres of the Almeria race he had to stop, his feet giving him more pain than his legs. The errant suitcase arrived, and reunited with his shoes, Chris prepared himself for the Tour of

Murcia which began the following day with a seven kilometre time trial, known in the cycling world as a 'prologue', and which decides the leader of the race for the first stage.

Chris started the prologue one minute behind the Dutch rider Eric Breukink who is regarded as one of the fastest time triallists in pro racing, and was the favourite for this stage. Chris beat him and the rest of the field, finishing 11 seconds in front of Breukink to take the yellow jersey of race leader. A winning margin of this size over such a short distance is unusual, particularly from a first year professional, but Chris kept his performance in perspective. 'I was really pleased to win, but most of the top guys were riding Paris-Nice, so I kept my feet on the ground about the significance of it.' Despite this he noticed that the attitudes of the other riders changed after his win in the prologue. 'I think it was a big breakthrough in other ways, almost as big as the hour record was. The hour put me in the position in the first place, but I think that the Murcia time trial will help me to get accepted.' He was in yellow, the sign of the leader – now he had to hold onto it, but with a GAN team not yet on full form it would be difficult.

Over the following two days, despite a below-par team, Chris kept his lead but problems arose on the fourth stage, when a 4,000-foot climb tested him to the limit. The Spanish rider Melchor Mauri, with the backing of a strong team, took the race apart over this mountain pass. Chris found himself left with one team-mate 30 seconds adrift from the leaders at the summit: 'I was in the right place at the right time, so it wasn't a tactical mistake – it was a physical thing. I just didn't have the legs to do it.' At the end of the stage Chris had lost the race leadership.

Despite losing the lead after three days, Chris doesn't see this as a prohibitive factor in his devel-

opment. 'They go so fast on the climbs, but once they've got the gap you can see them just 300 yards up the road, going the same speed as the chasers. I think I can make the transition as the season progresses. It might be the case that everyone else steps up a gear too, so we'll have to see.'

Chris turned his thoughts to the final stage of the race, an 11 kilometre time trial around the streets of Murcia. For the next two days he rode in the safety of the bunch, using the race as training, and preparing himself for the time trial. 'I was down as favourite for the final stage, but I was worried how I would go after five days' hard racing. I felt pressured, because everyone expected me to win, and obviously it mattered that I did.'

On the morning of the time trial Chris didn't have the chance to have his usual warm-up, but when he checked his pulse he knew that he had recovered from his efforts of the previous five days. Chris repeated his earlier prologue success, winning the time trial around the wide city centre roads, which were packed with spectators for the whole of the 11 kilometres. In his first major stage race for GAN, he had made his mark and sent a clear signal that he was the likely successor to the team leader, Greg LeMond. If Chris Boardman can develop his time trialling ability, and make up the deficit in the mountains, there will be no limit to what this rider can do.

Beyond Level Four?

ON 15 JANUARY 1994 FRANCESCO MOSER attempted to win back from Chris Boardman the world hour record he had blasted in Mexico 1984. He failed in his 10th–year anniversary record attempt. Just five minutes before Moser's attempt ended, Chris and Sally's third child, George, was born. The beginning of 1994 was certainly propitious.

The new year brought other changes: a new house was being built for the expanding Boardman family on the outskirts of Hoylake – not too far from the sea – and overlooking the Wirral countryside. This new home will be the base for Chris as he commutes around Europe earning his living from his sport, and it is the tangible evidence that he sees his family's future in Britain.

For this indefatigable cyclist, change has been the theme of the last two years. At the beginning of 1992 Chris was a talented bike rider whose name was only known really to other bike riders. Cycling is not a major sport in Great Britain, so Chris's 30 national titles, his countless wins in road and track races, and his performances in continental Europe meant nothing to the generally sports–crazy British public. But a combination of three key factors changed all that, and made Chris Boardman a household name in the summer of 1992.

ABOVE: *Peter Keen continues to work with Chris and has devised new training programmes for him to overcome the rigours of professional life.*

OPPOSITE: *Chris faces his biggest challenge now that he has turned professional. More road racing will inevitably push pursuiting and track racing down his list of priorities.*

Firstly there was the relentless drive and ambition of the man himself particularly with his ability to recover from the many race setbacks suffered over the years. Secondly, the training ideas and motivation skills of Peter Keen helped to hone and polish the raw talent that this sports scientist saw in the 18 year–old in 1987. Chris was transformed as a rider when he began using Keen's methods. But if he had won the Olympic title on a mere conventional bicycle, this alone would not have had such an impact on the collective British consciousness. What did make the impact was the ingenuity and engineering skills of Mike Burrows, the designer of revolutionary carbon fibre monocoque bicycle – the machine that became the third element in the success story of Chris Boardman.

The stunning sight of the LotusSport bike, the legend of the name, and the idea fanned by the media that a 'Superbike' could 'win' you a gold medal, catapulted Chris onto the front pages of

Chris joins Stuart Dangerfield (left) and Matthew Stephens (right), two new members of Chris's amateur club the North Wirral Velo, on a training ride in January 1994.

every national newspaper. For British cyclists his victory would become a reference point in their lives – a key date, as in 'before Chris won the gold' or 'after Chris won the gold'. Even for sports' fans generally, this would become a time when they would remember what they were doing when they heard the news, or who they were with when they watched it on television.

Boardman's Barcelona victory was especially significant because Britain had not won an Olympic cycling gold since 1922. British cycling fans were used to riders coming home with a suitcase full of hard luck stories and excuses. Chris Boardman changed all that in less than four and a

half minutes on a sunny evening in Spain.

In doing so he destroyed the myth that seems to have caused paralysis in many British cyclists when they race abroad – that riders from other countries are unbeatable, especially if they are the German Jens Lehmann. He was the world pursuit champion, a member of the all–conquering East German team, and the destroyer of Chris's world championship dream in 1991. But Barcelona changed all that. If Eddie Soens was looking down on that golden evening he would have been proud of Chris Boardman. Eddie had no time for the notion of foreign supermen: 'They've only got two arms, two legs and one 'ead, just like you', was his constant reminder to his riders. Chris proved that point as he caught and passed Lehmann. Even now, nearly two years later, it looks so easy on the video replay. Of course, it wasn't – it's just that great champions in any sport make what they do look easy.

But that was no flash-in-the-pan victory: that performance by Boardman had been 10 years in the making. From his first 10–mile race on that summer evening in 1982, Chris had progressed constantly, from just wanting to race, to setting club records and then eventually, winning races.

Chris Boardman has even admitted on a number of occasions that he doesn't really enjoy cycling. It's hard to believe, especially when one considers that Chris's background is in the grass roots sport of British time trialling, which delights in its low key, cosy, free-cup-of-tea atmosphere. But champions emerge from the unlikliest of places and while at one time it might have appeared that Chris was happy to settle for the meagre rewards and modest acclaim of a UK time trial 'star', deep down was a born winner who one day would inevitably seek victory against the best cyclists in the world.

For it's the winning, not a love of cycling, that drives a man like Boardman, and in professional sport today, that's the number one qualification. It is the need to progress that drives Chris, and that need was only temporarily satisfied in Barcelona. As Boardman himself has said, when one goal is reached, he looks immediately for the next one. He is a man who enjoys winning, but who hates losing even more. Such a nature could be destructive

because it is not easy, or possible, to win every time.

And when Boardman is beaten, he can handle it. He can deal with the intensity of the disappointment, and in what is probably his greatest strength, he analyzes the reasons for his defeat. This is the aspect of Chris Boardman that his manager, Peter Woodworth, admires most of all. 'His ability to pick himself up from the depths of despair amazes me. I've seen him at his absolute lowest, when most people would be inclined to say "I've had enough" and he's come back from that, and turned out a world class performance.'

Chris's dislike of losing does not include the smaller races that he is sometimes obliged to ride, both to honour his contract and as a part of his training. The races he has targeted for this current year also happen to be the aim of the best riders in the world, so the competition will be intense. Some racing pundits might argue that a first year professional shouldn't aim so high – that Chris should have a steady first season before he starts thinking about the Grand Prix des Nations or the World Championship time trial. However, it is precisely because Chris aims so high that he is in the position that he is in today. If he believes that he has a realistic chance of achieving a goal, he will put everything into working towards it.

This has always been his way. Back in November 1991 he was asked to make a speech at a local cycling club's prize presentation, and he began with a message to the younger members of the club, telling them to aim for something – a local championship or whatever they wanted to achieve – and then stick to that aim, even if they were told that they could not do it. In a reference to the tests that he had as an 18 year old, he told the audience 'I was told that I wouldn't make a pursuit rider; that it wasn't physically possible for me to get to the top...but I thought, "well, I like pursuiting, and I really want to do it, so I'm going to carry on with it".'

And he did carry on. Eight months later he was Olympic champion, guided and trained by the man who had made that original assessment, but then changed it as his ideas on pursuit preparation developed – Peter Keen. Peter is constantly re-assessing Chris's potential and predicts that Chris will become one of the top road-racers in the world over the next three to five years, and as a consequence will move away from the track and short-distance races he has dominated until now.

'In his career to date' says Keen, 'Chris has been most successful at events lasting between 4 minutes and 2 hours, ie., races over 2.5 to 60 miles. Given such a range of time and distance it may come as a surprise to many that Chris is widely seen as a short-distance specialist rather than an all-rounder. However, the athletic qualities required to be successful over this range of distances are remarkably similar, and are some-what different to the physiological and psychological strengths required for success in professional continental road racing, where races last many hours and are often staged over several days. To succeed in such races a rider needs to be able to burn fat very efficiently and to resist rises in body temperature, as well as absorb the daily pounding the body receives.

'In simple terms, Chris currently has a very powerful engine, but one that is un-economical in terms of "fuel" consumption, and is not very resistant to wear and tear. It also has a tendency to over heat! Thankfully, this situation simply reflects the specialised training that he has done in the past. In the future his programme will evolve in order to develop the "endurance" he will need to conquer the highest peaks the sport has to offer – the One-Day Classics and the three Tours – France, Italy

and Spain. Can he do this? Well, as a coach I believe it is easier to fine-tune a big, powerful engine than get more power out of a fine-tuned small engine.

'But professional road cycling is not simply about having the best engine. One needs exceptional bike-handling skills and a great deal of tactical and psychological strength in order to win. The supreme road-racer is therefore a blend of marathon runner, motorcyclist and chess player! To become such an individual, Chris Boardman will need to learn a great deal in a short time. The challenge will tax his reserves of ambition and motivation to the limit, but his capacity for learning is immense and I believe he will succeed. Chris has an open, enquiring mind – he enjoys challenging dogma and there is plenty of it in sport!'

Chris acknowledges the debt that he owes Peter Keen, whose training levels have played their part in Chris's success. Level Four is the furthest a rider can go on Keen's scale of training, and it is perhaps a signal of intent that the name of Chris Boardman's company is Beyond Level Four.

Since winning that gold medal there have been many changes to Chris's life: First of all there was the 'media lifestyle' which had him appearing regularly in newspapers, magazines and on television, including the BBC Sports Personality Award which saw him sitting with the contenders on the front row – the closest a racing cyclist has been to taking the award since the late Tom Simpson won it in 1965. Further recognition followed when Chris was awarded the MBE in the New Year Honours list for his Olympic victory.

But not all of the forecast changes have taken place. In the days immediately after Barcelona there were some headlines which informed the world that Chris would 'earn a million'. These were just a little off the mark. He has negotiated a

good contract with GAN, and in financial terms the immediate future looks secure enough, but his Olympic title has not been a passport to a life of untold riches, as the tabloid headlines would have had us believe.

The Boardman-Obree rivalry was also somewhat hyped by the media, although Chris could never have predicted the impact that Graeme Obree would have on his plans for the hour record and the world championship. As Graeme himself readily acknowledges: 'Because we'd been stuck on the same island for so long, the rivalry did build up; but now we're at world level it won't be as intense – unless the hour record sucks us back in again.' Whether or not that happens, Obree is gracious about his 'rival': 'Chris's overriding strength, apart from his speed, is his consistency. You can rely on the fact that whenever he races he has prepared meticulously. Every time I've raced

Greg LeMond (above) is Boardman's only English-speaking team-mate on the GAN squad. The veteran American triple Tour winner has been impressed by Chris's progress since signing for the French team.

against him I've known I've had to be at my very very best because Chris rarely has an off day.'

Winning is Chris's number one motivator and his post-hour record and early pro performance has been an impressive one. His victory in the Eddy Merckx GP, fourth place in the GP des Nations and so far in 1994, his victories in the time trial stages of the Tour of Murcia, have made everyone involved in professional cycling sit up and take notice of the man from Hoylake.

Greg LeMond, the triple Tour de France winner and twice World Champion, has been impressed by Chris's achievements, and is in no doubt about the potential of the man. 'I think say, 90 percent of the pros in the *peloton*. The big improvements will come with better training habits, which Chris seems to be aware of.'

LeMond says he'll be watching with interest to see how Chris does against the other top riders in the time trial stages. 'A lot of the guys were talking about going for the hour record after they saw two amateurs get it last year,' he says. 'Since Chris won the time trials at Murcia they will have had second thoughts, and if he consistently beats them they'll realize he has more talent than they originally thought.'

This is praise indeed from the man who Chris has singled out as the rider he most admires. Others too can see a golden future for Chris. Among them is Doug Dailey, the British track coach, who acknowledges that while Chris's future is in road racing, he sees him as a contender for the gold medal at

The Manchester velodrome during building work in March 1994 – the venue for future hour record attempts?

Chris has a really big future, and I said so to Roger Legeay last year,' says LeMond.

LeMond believes that the qualities which enabled Chris to win the Olympics and take the Hour record will allow him to be a Tour de France contender in two or three years' time, and that Chris's approach to racing and training will ensure a successful career. 'In Peter Keen, Chris has an excellent trainer. He has come into professional cycle racing with more knowledge than, I would

the next Olympics in Atlanta in 1996. 'Hopefully I'll have Chris on the squad for Atlanta,' says Dailey. 'On present form and allowing for that to continue, we could see him in the final of the pursuit again.'

Peter Woodworth sees Chris's future as one of steady progression: 'In 1995 and 1996 I think we'll see Chris establishing himself as a top rider in Europe.' As for whether or not Chris will ride the Tour de France in the future, Peter says only this, 'There's no point in going to the Tour just for the experience and coming home a broken man. But if he hits really good form, then that's different.'

Peter Keen knows this too, but is aware of the scale of it all: 'We have to start again to prepare for the next challenges, I've said that you don't need paratrooper-type training to be a bike rider, but it may be a paratrooper mentality that gets you through the Tour de France – we don't know yet.'

Chris has always taken his sport very seriously — he rarely cycles without a pulse monitor or carefully measured ration of energy drink, even on a winter mountain bike trip to Wales — but in the past his goals have been obscured. The Olympics and hour record, however, brought the future sharply into focus, and turning professional has opened up a whole new chapter on his career. He's already tasted success, that's important, and now he needs to settle into his new life before realizing his full potential.

Chris is now approaching his best years as a cyclist. The mid 20s to early 30s are prime years for physical form, experience and ambition and he has already shown the mental drive to succeed. All he needs now is a balanced programme with time to rest and build up for specific targets. Only then will we see if Chris is capable of going beyond Level Four. But for now, the words of the ultimate cyclist in Chris's eyes, Greg LeMond, say it all.

'I think that anyone who can ride 52 kilometres in an hour at sea level is capable of doing anything he wants to in professional cycling.'

Part two of the Boardman story is only just beginning.

The Boardmans have close links with the Wirral, a place it seems Chris will always return to. The incentive to provide for his growing family is a very real spur for him. Sally and their children will be living in Hoylake while Chris packs his suitcase and travels all over Europe.

The Reference Section

WORLD HOUR RECORD HOLDERS

KEY – (a) Denotes amateur rider, otherwise record breakers were professional (B) Belgium; (DK) Denmark; (F) France; (GB) Great Britain; (I) Italy; (NL) Holland; (Switz) Switzerland ; + Above 600 metres above sea level; - Below 600 metres above sea level

DATE	NAME	WHERE	RECORD (km)
11.05.1893	Henri Desgrange (F) (a)	(-) Paris-Buffalo	35.325
31.10.1894	Jules Dubois (F)	(-) Paris-Buffalo	38.220
30.07.1897	Oscar Ven Den Eynde (B)	(-) Paris-Cipale	39.240
9.07.1898	Willie Hamilton (USA)	(+) Denver	40.781
24.08.1905	Lucien Petit-Breton (F)	(-) Paris-Buffalo	41.110
20.06.1907	Marcel Berthet (F) (a)	(-) Paris-Buffalo	41.520
22.08.1912	Oscar Egg (Switz)	(-) Paris-Buffalo	42.360
7.08.1913	Marcel Berthet (F) (a)	(-) Paris-Buffalo	42.741
21.08.1913	Oscar Egg (Switz)	(-) Paris-Buffalo	43.525
20.09.1913	Marcel Berthet (F) (a)	(-) Paris-Buffalo	43.775
18.06.1914	Oscar Egg (Switz)	(-) Paris-Buffalo	44.247
25.08.1933	Jan Van Hout (NL)	(-) Roermond	44.588
29.08.1933	Maurice Richard (F)	(-) Sint Truiden	44.777
31.10.1935	Giuseppe Olmo (I)	(-) Milan-Vigorelli	45.067
14.10.1936	Maurice Richard (F)	(-) Milan-Vigorelli	45.375
29.09.1937	Frans Slaats (NL)	(-) Milan-Vigorelli	45.535
3.11.1937	Maurice Archambaud (F)	(-) Milan-Vigorelli	45.817
7.11.1942	Fausto Coppi (I)	(-) Milan-Vigorelli	45.848
29.06.1956	Jacques Anquetil (F)	(-) Milan-Vigorelli	46.159
19.09.1956	Ercole Baldini (I) (a)	(-) Milan-Vigorelli	46.393
18.09.1957	Roger Riviere (F)	(-) Milan-Vigorelli	46.923
23.09.1958	Roger Riviere (F)	(-) Milan-Vigorelli	47.346
30.10.1967	Ferdinand Bracke (B)	(-) Rome-Olympic	48.093
10.10.1968	Ole Ritter (DK)	(+) Mexico-Olympic	48.653
25.10.1972	Eddy Merckx (B)	(+) Mexico-Olympic	49.431
19.01.1984	Francesco Moser (I)	(+) Mexico-Olympic	50.808
23.01.1984	Francesco Moser (I)	(+) Mexico-Olympic	51.151
17.07.1993	Graeme Obree (GB) (a)	(-) Hamar-Viking Ship	51.596
23.07.1993	Chris Boardman (GB) (a)	(-) Bordeaux-Le Lac	52.270

THE GREAT WORLD HOUR RECORD HOLDERS

HENRI DESGRANGE
(b: 31.01.1865. d: 16.08.1940)

The Frenchman who went on to found the Tour de France, which began in 1903, set many world records on the old cement Buffalo track in Paris. Establishing the hour record was done on a bicycle weighing 33lbs – more than twice the weight of the modern machine.

MAURICE ARCHAMBAUD
(b: 30.08.1906. d: 3.12.1955)

It took Archambaud five attempts to break the hour record. The first time he tried was in 1932 when he covered 44.564km on the Paris-Buffalo track only to find that the timekeeper had not been agreed by the governing body, the *Union Cycliste Internationale*, so it was not approved. Then followed three attempts on Italy's famous Vigorelli velodrome, all ending with punctures in the October of 1937. In the following November on the same track, he finally set new record figures.

FAUSTO COPPI
(b: 15.09.1919. d: 21.01.1960)

Next to Eddy Merckx, Coppi is seen as the greatest ever rider, and the Italian legend raced as a professional for 19 years, winning most of the world's famous races. He died from malaria after returning home from a holiday in the High Volta with Anquetil, Riviere, Raphael Geminiani, Henri Anglade and Roger Hassenforder – all famous riders of the period.

JACQUES ANQUETIL
(b: 8.01.1934. d: 18.11.1987)

The finest rider ever against the watch, Maître Jacques, won the Tour de France five times, and his hour record came 14 years after Coppi,

taking it into the 46-kilometre bracket. He was awarded France's highest honour, the *Chevalier de la Légion d'Honneur* in 1966.

ERCOLE BALDINI
(b: 26.01.1933)

The last amateur to break the record until Graeme Obree in 1993, Baldini will never forget 1956, as he also became the world 4,000 metres pursuit champion (at this time, it was not an Olympic event) and the Olympic road race champion in Melbourne. He later became the first Olympic champion also to win the world professional road race title (1958).

ROGER RIVIERE
(b: 23.02.1936. d: 1.04.1976)

A rider very much in the mould of Chris Boardman, Riviere was soaked in natural speed and his hour record was eagerly awaited. Sadly, his professional career lasted only three years, ruined by a crash when he plunged off the col du Perjuret during the 1960 Tour de France. It ended his career and he died from cancer of the throat at the age of 40.

OLE RITTER
(b: 29.08.1941)

Ritter became a hero in Denmark after he beat Riviere's record by going to Mexico in 1968 for the first altitude attempt since Willie Hamilton in 1898. After Eddy Merckx beat his distance four years later, Ritter returned to try again, but failed.

EDDY MERCKX
(b: 17.06.1945)

The cycling world awaited January 1972 to see what the Belgian supremo could do to Ritter's hour record. The answer was more than 49 kilometres, but he did not reach the magical 50 kilometres barrier. When Moser broke Merckx's record 11 years later, it was the subject of a protest from Belgium because they felt Moser's equipment had taken his machine outside the rules.

FRANCESCO MOSER
(b: 19.06.1951)

An athlete of outstanding vintage – Moser became the first rider to beat the 50 kilometre barrier, riding at altitude. After Boardman broke the record, Moser returned from a long retirement in January 1994 to better his record. Although he failed to reach Boardman's record, he did beat

Obree's figures despite being almost 43 years old – an achievement confirming the Italian still possessed the heart of a lion.

TACTICS TO TAKE THE HOUR

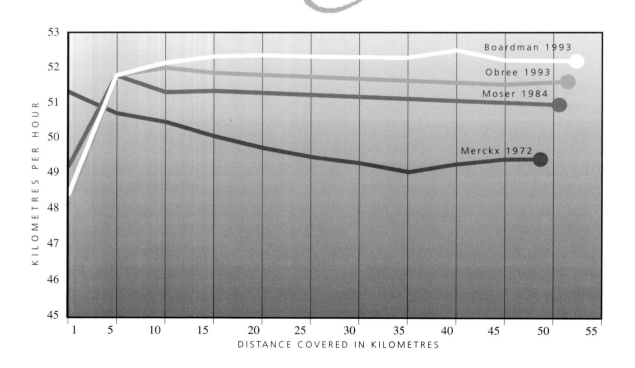

THE GRAPH above compares the speeds of the last four record holders measured at 5km intervals. Notice how Eddy Merckx's speed begins high, drops steadily and then increases dramatically as he nears the end of the hour. Compare this to the tactics of later riders.

124

CHRIS BOARDMAN'S RACING HIGHLIGHTS 1984-1994

1984
National Schoolboy
Championship, 10 miles.

1985
Gold Medal National Team
Pursuit Championship.
(At 16, the youngest person ever
to be selected to represent Great
Britain at senior level at World
Championships in Italy.)
Represented GB at Junior World
Championships in West Germany.

1986
Gold Medal National Junior
25 mile Championship.
National Junior best all-rounder.
Gold Medal National Team
Pursuit Championships.
Represented GB at World
Championships in Colorado, USA,
in individual and team pursuits.
Bronze Medal Winner Team
Pursuit, Commonwealth Games,
Edinburgh.

1987
Represented GB at World
Championships in Austria, in the
team pursuit.
Gold Medal National Team
Pursuit Championships (record
time).
Silver Medal National Hill Climb
Championship.
Gold Medal National Hill Climb
Championship (wining team).

1988
Gold Medal Road Time Trial
Association 100km Team Time
Trial.
Gold Medal National Team
Pursuit Championships.
Silver Medal BCF 100km Team
Time Trial.
Silver Medal National Individual
Pursuit.
Gold Medal National Hill Climb
Championship (winning team).

1st Grand Prix of France
International Time Trial.
Track Cycling Team Captain for
GB in Seoul Olympic Games.

1989
Senior National
25 mile Champion.
Gold Medal National 25 mile
Championship Team.
Gold Medal Road Time Trials
Association 100km Team Time
Trial.
Gold Medal BCF 100km Team
Time Trial (fastest time recorded
by a British team anywhere).
Gold Medal National Individual
Pursuit.
Gold Medal National Team Pursuit.
Gold Medal National Hill Climb
Championship (winning team).

1990
Bronze Medal Winner Team
Pursuit, Commonwealth Games,
New Zealand.
Bronze Medal Winner Team Time
Trial, Commonwealth Games,
New Zealand.
Gold Medal National 25 mile
Time Trial (winning team).
Silver Medal National Individual
Pursuit.
Best British Rider (qualified 7th
fastest Individual Pursuit, finished
9th Individual Points Race) World
Track Championships, Japan.
1st in all three October Classic
Mountain Time Trials.
Fastest 50 mile time trial of the
year.
Broke 12-year-old 50-mile team
record.

Other notable records 1984-1990
Junior National Record Holder at
25 miles – 52 minutes, 9 seconds
(aged 15).
Winner Isle of Man International
Mountain Time Trial on TT
Course 1987, 1989.

Winner Circuit of the Dales
Classic 50 mile Time Trial 1987
and 1989.
4-times Winner Merseyside
Wheelers Circuit of Delamere
Pro/Am Classic.
Winner Porthole Grand Prix
Pro/Am Classic Time Trial.
Represented GB at Senior level
since 15 years of age.
Stage Winner Tour of Lancashire
Pro/Am (3rd overall best
amateur).
1st Douglas International
Criterium.
Stage Winner Tour of Texas 1990.

1991
24 wins
1st National 25 mile Time Trial
Championship (record time).
1st National 50 mile Time Trial
Championship.
1st 100km Team Time Trial
Championship BCF (record time).
1st 100km Team Time Trial
Championship RTTC.
1st Individual Pursuit
Championship (record time).
1st Team Pursuit Championship.
2nd Pre-Olympic meeting Team
Pursuit, Barcelona.
5th Qualifier World
Championship Pursuit, Stuttgart.
1st National Hill Climb
Championship.
World Amateur 5km record –
5 minutes, 47.70 seconds.
1st Hope Valley Classic Star
Trophy .
1st Pro/Am Tour of Lancashire.
(Numerous Classic wins.)

1992 (short season)
1st (10 times).
2nd (3 times).
3rd (twice).
Olympic Gold Medal (and
Olympic record).
World Record.
World 5km record attempt.

CHRIS BOARDMAN'S RACING HIGHLIGHTS 1984-1994(cont.)

5th Olympic Team Pursuit. National Individual Pursuit Champion and National 4km record. National 25 and 50 mile Championship and Championship Team. National 25 mile record – 47 minutes, 19 seconds. 1st stage 1 Prologue, Circuit des Mines, France

1993
1st (22 times).
2nd (8 times).
4th (once).

World 1 Hour record – 52.270km. 3rd World Individual Pursuit Championships. 1st 25 mile Time Trial Championship (Team and Championship record). 1st National Team Time Trial Championship (Championship record). 1st Isle of Man Time Trial (course record). 1st Tour of Lancashire Pro/Am. 25 mile Time Trial record – 45 minutes, 57 seconds

Professional Debut 1993/94
1st Grand Prix Eddy Merckx, Belgium. 2nd Baden-Baden Telekom '2 Up' Time Trial with Claudio Chiappucci. 1st Duo-Normand with Laurent Bezault, France. 1st Chrono des Herbiers, France. 4th Grand Prix des Nations, France. 1st Milimetro del Corsa, Venice, Italy. 2nd Forenza-Pistoria, Italy.

GLOSSARY

Aerodynamics An area which concerns all racing cyclists who wish to improve their performance by reducing 'drag'. It involves the study especially of the forces which act on a body passing through air, and thereby aims to improve the performance of that body, be it a plane or bike.

BCF British Cycling Federation. The governing body of cycling in Britain. The federal system has national and local representation, with the country being split into Divisions.

Carbon fibre A thread of pure carbon which because of its strength and lightness is used to reinforce cycling components and frames, as well as many other everyday items.

Derailleur Mechanism that moves the chain up and down the block.

Disc wheel Solid-sided wheel with hollow or braced interior used in time trials.

Domestique Team rider who rides in support of a team leader by fetching and carrying drinks and clothing, and chases or defends the leader's position on the road.

Green jersey Award normally given to the leader of a road race on points – usually won by the most consistent sprinter rather than the overall leader.

Hill climb An uphill time trial, over anything from about 600 yards to 3 miles. The riders battle against gravity as well as the clock in these popular races, held during autumn. The British championship is on a different hill each year at the end of October, and thousands come from all over the country to see the spectacle.

HPV Human Powered Vehicle. Any chain-driven, pedal-powered machine which does not fall into the UCI definition of a bicycle is known as an HPV.

Index gears Method of shifting the gears by a click system of synchronized gear levers and derailleur. Known as SIS by Japanese manufacturer Shimano.

King of the Mountains Title given to the best hill climber in a road race. In the Tour de France he wears a white jersey with red polka dots.

Low profile Term for 'droop snoop' time-trial bike, often fitted with a small front wheel and aerodynamic handlebars.

Monocoque In this case a bicycle frame constructed from carbon fibre in a single structure, instead of the usual separate steel tubes, which are welded together to form the frame shape.

Obree position The riding style favoured by Graeme Obree which he began using in the late 1980s and which was ridiculed by many until his hour record and world championship victory demanded a re-assessment of the man and his methods. Francesco Moser adopted the Obree position for his attempt on the 'hour', while Chris Boardman also used it in trials during the winter of 1993-94. The UCI outlawed such a riding position for road use in January 1994, on safety grounds, and it is under review for track use.

Open race Race contested by professionals and amateurs.

Peloton French for bunch (of cycling racers).

Pursuit race Held on a velodrome, two riders start on opposite sides of the track, with the object of closing the distance on each other over 4,000 metres for the men's race, or 3,000 metres for the women's event.

Rainbow jersey White, with horizontal rainbow bands, this jersey signifies a cycling world champion in any of the disciplines recognized by the UCI, and is perhaps the most coveted of all cycling's symbolic jerseys.

Road race A race which takes place on the road, and in which all the competitors start together. The winner is the first rider over the line. Tactics play a role in these races, which usually range between 30 to 140 miles.

Schedule A race plan which the rider uses in order to achieve the desired time. Before the race begins, rider and trainer will work out the schedule, and the rider will be kept informed if they are ahead of, or behind, the target time.

Six Day race At indoor velodromes throughout Europe, from Bordeaux to Moscow, cycling fans can see the stars of professional racing at close quarters between the months of September and March. In teams of two, the riders amass points to decide the winners over the six days, competing in all forms of track cycling in these showcase events.

Stage Daily race in a stage race.

Time trial Individual race against the clock.

Toe clips Metal clips mounted on the pedals into which the foot slips. Less common among professional road racers nowadays as most use quick-release pedals.

Track race Any race which takes place on the velodrome, or occasionally on grass tracks, ranging in distance from the 800-metre sprint, to the 20 kilometre race, and of course, the hour record.

Training effect The means by which the body develops, through intensive training and exercise, and is able to cope better with the rigours of racing.

Tri-spoke wheel The corollary of the disc wheel. The tri-spoke, built from carbon fibre, is thought to have more aerodynamic qualities than the solid disc, and does not give the rider the disconcerting buffeting in sidewinds that its predecessor does.

Triathlon bars Narrow bars that are bolted onto normal handlebars, enabling the rider to assume an elbows-in position for time trialling.

Tubular Lightweight racing tyre that is completely round and sealed, with stitching and glue. Usually known as a 'tub'.

UCI *Union Cycliste Internationale*. The world cycling body which governs all road and track, amateur and professional cycling racing.

Velodrome Banked circuit for track racing, made from wood, concrete or asphalt.

Yellow jersey The symbol of the race leader in a stage race. The yellow jersey, or *maillot jaune*, was the idea of Henri Desgrange, the founder of the Tour de France. The sponsor of the race was a newspaper, *L'Auto*, which was printed on yellow paper, hence the colour of the jersey. In Italy the national tour is sponsored by a journal printed on pink paper, so the *maglia rosa*, the pink jersey, identifies the race leader.

ACKNOWLEDGEMENTS

*"For Sally-Anne Boardman, a woman I lean on far too much, and
without whom the material for this book would never have existed."*

CHRIS BOARDMAN

SPECIAL THANKS

THE AUTHORS would like to thank Sally-Anne Boardman, Keith and
Carol Boardman, Ann and Rosanna Bell, Mike Bell, Mike Burrows, Muriel
Coutourier, Doug Dailey, Alan Dunn, Mick Jagger, Peter Keen, Greg LeMond,
Catherine Mackrell, Harry Middleton, Graeme Obree, Anne O'Hare, Bob
Prince, Jacques Suer, Bill Soens, Mima Soens, Bill Warren, Patrick Peal and
Richard Hill from Lotus, Dave Voller and particular thanks to Peter Woodworth.

FORMER RACING CYCLIST Antony Bell (pictured above with Peter
Woodworth [left] and Chris [right]) who researched and co-wrote
this book, had moderate success on the road and once finished second in a
38-mile race to the then 16 year-old Chris Boardman. 'When Chris became a
top class rider' says Antony, 'I regaled everybody who would listen with the
story of how I shared the lead with the man who went on to be Olympic
champion. In the course of researching this book, I was somewhat perplexed
to discover that Chris had no recollection of this race(!) which to him was an
insignificant step on his way to the top honours. Even then, in March 1985, it
was clear to me that Chris Boardman was destined for much greater achievements.' Now a freelance writer and political researcher based in the Wirral,
Antony is married to Ann and has a baby daughter, Rosanna – born
during the production of this book.

PICTURE CREDITS

Allsport/Chris Cole: front cover. Agence France Presse: 8.
The Associated Press Ltd : 9. BBC: 10,26,27,32,35. Paul Cox: 6.
Cycling Weekly: 19 (r), 20, 42, 71, 72. Deutsche Presse-Agentur/Press
Association Ltd: 11. Alan Dunn: 85. Chris Lees: 24. Ken Matthews: 19(l).
Harry Maylin: 74. Olympia/Colorsport: 70. Bob Prince: 16. Hans-Alfred
Roth: 25,40,44. Bernard Thompson: 21. Len Thorpe: 17. United Press
Photos: 73. Graham Watson: 14,43,51,53, 54/55,56,90,91,93,95,97,98,99.
Phil O'Connor: all other photographs.